CW00493953

Chartered Insti
Management Accou

This book comes with free EN-gage online resources so that you can study anytime, anywhere. This free online resource is not sold separately and is included in the price of the book.

How to access your online resources

You can access additional online resources associated with this CIMA Official book via the EN-gage website at: **www.EN-gage.co.uk/addabook**.

Existing users

If you are an **existing EN-gage user**, simply log-in to your account using the address above, which will enable you to use the 'add a book' menu. Enter the ISBN of this book and the unique pass key number in the scratch panel below to gain access to the extra online products.

New users

If you are a new EN-gage user then you will first need to register at: **www.EN-gage.co.uk**. Once registered, Kaplan Publishing will send you an email containing a link to activate your account - please check your junk mail if you do not receive this or contact us using the details printed on the back cover of this book. Click on the link to activate your account.

To unlock your additional resources, go to **www.EN-gage.co.uk/addabook**. You will then need to enter the ISBN of this book (found on page ii or the back cover) and the unique pass key number contained in the scratch panel below:

Then click 'finished' or 'add another book'.

Please allow 24 hours from the time you submit your book details for the content to appear in your account.

Your code and information

This code can only be used once for the registration of one book online. This registration will expire when this edition of the book is no longer current - please see the back cover of this book for the expiry date.

Using your online resources during your studies

All of the free online resources have been designed to support your studies. The extra online testing provides valuable question practice prior to your assessment and therefore we strongly recommend using this alongside this book.

KAPLAN PUBLISHING

BA4

FUNDAMENTALS OF ETHICS, CORPORATE GOVERNANCE AND BUSINESS LAW

CIMA EXAM PRACTICE KIT

CIMA PUBLISHING

KAPLAN PUBLISHING

Published by: Kaplan Publishing UK

Unit 2 The Business Centre, Molly Millars Lane, Wokingham, Berkshire RG41 2QZ

Copyright © 2016 Kaplan Financial Limited. All rights reserved.

No part of this publication may be reproduced, stored in a retrieval system or transmitted in any form or by any means electronic, mechanical, photocopying, recording or otherwise without the prior written permission of the publisher.

Acknowledgements

We are grateful to the CIMA for permission to reproduce past examination questions.

Notice

The text in this material and any others made available by any Kaplan Group company does not amount to advice on a particular matter and should not be taken as such. No reliance should be placed on the content as the basis for any investment or other decision or in connection with any advice given to third parties. Please consult your appropriate professional adviser as necessary. Kaplan Publishing Limited and all other Kaplan group companies expressly disclaim all liability to any person in respect of any losses or other claims, whether direct, indirect, incidental, consequential or otherwise arising in relation to the use of such materials.

British Library Cataloguing in Publication Data
A catalogue record for this book is available from the British Library

ISBN: 978-1-78415-764-7

Printed and bound in Great Britain.

CONTENTS

Quality and accuracy are of the utmost importance to us so if you spot an error in any of our products, please send an email to mykaplanreporting@kaplan.com with full details.

Our Quality Co-ordinator will work with our technical team to verify the error and take action to ensure it is corrected in future editions.

INDEX TO QUESTIONS AND ANSWERS

OBJECTIVE TEST QUESTIONS

SYLLABUS GUIDANCE, LEARNING OBJECTIVES AND VERBS

A THE CERTIFICATE IN BUSINESS ACCOUNTING (CERT BA)

The Cert BA provides a foundation in the essential elements of accounting and business. This includes the Fundamentals of Ethics, Corporate Governance and Business Law. There are four subject areas, which are all tested by computer-based assessment (CBA). The four subjects are:

- BA1: Fundamentals of Business Economics
- BA2: Fundamentals of Management Accounting
- BA3: Fundamentals of Financial Accounting
- BA4: Fundamentals of Ethics, Corporate Governance and Business Law

The Cert BA is both a qualification in its own right and an entry route to the next stage in CIMA's examination structure.

The examination structure after the Certificate comprises:

- Operational Level
- Management Level
- Strategic Level

The CIMA Qualification includes more advanced topics in Accounting and Business. It is therefore very important that you apply yourself to Fundamentals of Ethics, Corporate Governance and Business Law, not only because it is part of the Certificate, but also as a platform for more advanced studies. It is thus an important step in becoming a qualified member of the Chartered Institute of Management Accountants.

B AIMS OF THE SYLLABUS

The aims of the syllabus are

- to provide for the Institute, together with the practical experience requirements, an adequate basis for assuring society that those admitted to membership are competent to act as management accountants for entities, whether in manufacturing, commercial or service organisations, in the public or private sectors of the economy;
- to enable the Institute to examine whether prospective members have an adequate knowledge, understanding and mastery of the stated body of knowledge and skills;
- to complement the Institute's practical experience and skills development requirements.

C STUDY WEIGHTINGS

A percentage weighting is shown against each topic in the syllabus. This is intended as a guide to the proportion of study time each topic requires.

All topics in the syllabus must be studied, since any single examination question may examine more than one topic, or carry a higher proportion of marks than the percentage study time suggested.

The weightings do not specify the number of marks that will be allocated to topics in the examination.

D CIMA'S HIERARCHY OF LEARNING OBJECTIVES

CIMA places great importance on the definition of verbs in structuring Objective Test Examinations. It is therefore crucial that you understand the verbs in order to appreciate the depth and breadth of a topic and the level of skill required. The CIMA Cert BA syllabus learning outcomes and objective test questions will focus on levels one, two and three of the CIMA's hierarchy of learning objectives (knowledge, comprehension and application). However, as you progress to the Operational, Management and Strategic levels of the CIMA Professional Qualification, testing will include levels four and five of the hierarchy. As you complete your CIMA Professional Qualification, you can therefore expect to be tested on knowledge, comprehension, application, analysis and evaluation.

In CIMA Cert BA Objective Test Examinations you will meet verbs from only levels 1, 2, and 3 of the hierarchy which are as follows:

Level 1: KNOWLEDGE

What you are expected to know

VERBS USED	DEFINITION
List	Make a list of.
State	Express, fully or clearly, the details/facts of.
Define	Give the exact meaning of.

For example you could be asked to define economic terms such as 'inflation' (BA1), or to define the term 'management accounting' (BA2) or to state the accounting entries required to record the revaluation surplus arising on revaluation of land and buildings (BA3).

Level 2: COMPREHENSION

What you are expected to understand

VERBS USED	DEFINITION
Describe	Communicate the key features of.
Distinguish	Highlight the differences between.
Explain	Make clear or intelligible/state the meaning or purpose of.
Identify	Recognise, establish or select after consideration.
Illustrate	Use an example to describe or explain something.

For example you could be asked to explain the components of the circular flow of funds (BA1), or distinguish between financial accounting and management accounting (BA3) or distinguish between express terms and implied terms of a contract of employment (BA4).

Level 3: APPLICATION

How you are expected to apply your knowledge

VERBS USED	DEFINITION
Apply	Put to practical use.
Calculate	Ascertain or reckon mathematically.
Demonstrate	Exhibit by practical means.
Prepare	Make or get ready for use.
Reconcile	Make or prove consistent/compatible.
Solve	Find an answer to or prove with certainty.
Tabulate	Arrange in a table.

For example you could be asked to reconcile the differences between profits calculated using absorption costing and marginal costing (BA2), or to calculate the gain or loss on disposal of a noncurrent asset (BA3) or to apply relevant principles to determine the outcome of a law-based or ethical problem (BA4).

For reference, levels 4 and 5 of the hierarchy require demonstration of analysis and evaluation skills respectively. Further detail on levels 4 and 5 of the hierarchy which are tested in the CIMA Professional Qualification can be obtained from the CIMA website.

OBJECTIVE TESTS

Objective Test questions require you to choose or provide a response to a question whose correct answer is predetermined.

The most common types of Objective Test question you will see are:

- **multiple choice**, where you have to choose the correct answer(s) from a list of possible answers - this could either be numbers or text
- **multiple response** with more choices and answers, for example, choosing two correct answers from a list of five available answers - this could either be numbers or text
- **number entry**, where you give your numeric answer to one or more parts of a question, for example, gross profit is $25,000 and the accrual for heat and light charges is $750
- **drag and drop**, where you match one or more items with others from the list available, for example, matching several accounting terms with the appropriate definition
- **drop down**, where you choose the correct answer from those available in a drop down menu, for example, choosing the correct calculation of an accounting ratio, or stating whether an individual statement is true or false. This can also be included with a number entry style question
- **hot spot**, where, for example, you use your computer cursor or mouse to identify an area of specific location on an image (e.g. graph) by clicking on it

CIMA has provided the following guidance relating to the format of questions and their marking:

- questions which require narrative responses to be typed will not be used
- for number entry questions, clear guidance will usually be given about the format in which the answer is required e.g. "to the nearest $" or "to two decimal places"
- item set questions provide a scenario which then forms the basis of more than one question (usually between 2 and 4 questions). These sets of questions would appear together in the test and are most likely to appear in BA2 and BA3
- all questions are independent so that, where questions are based on a common item set scenario, each question will be distinct and the answer to a later question will not be dependent upon answering an earlier question correctly
- all items are equally weighted and, where a question consists of more than one element, all elements must be answered correctly for the question to be marked correct.

Throughout this Exam Practice Kit we have introduced these types of questions, but we have had to label answers A, B, C etc. rather than using click boxes. For convenience we have retained quite a few questions where an initial scenario leads to a number of sub-questions. There will be questions of this type in the Objective Test Examination but they will rarely have more than three sub-questions.

Guidance re CIMA on-screen calculator

As part of the CIMA Objective Test software, candidates are provided with a calculator. This calculator is on-screen and is available for the duration of the assessment. The calculator is available in Objective Test Examinations for BA1, BA2 and BA3 (it is not required for BA4).

Guidance regarding calculator use in the Objective Test Examinations is available online at: https://connect.cimaglobal.com/

CIMA Cert BA Objective Tests

The Objective Tests are a two-hour assessment comprising compulsory questions, each with one or more parts. There will be no choice and all questions should be attempted. The number of questions in each assessment are as follows:

BA1 Fundamentals of Business Economics – 60 questions

BA2 Fundamentals of Management Accounting – 60 questions

BA3 Fundamentals of Financial Accounting-– 60 questions

BA4 Fundamentals of Ethics, Corporate Governance and Business Law – 85 questions

SYLLABUS OUTLINE

BA4

FUNDAMENTALS OF ETHICS, CORPORATE GOVERNANCE AND BUSINESS LAW

Syllabus overview

The learning outcomes in this subject reflect the professional standards to be demonstrated for the benefit of all stakeholders. With this in mind, the place of ethics and ethical conflict is an essential underpinning for commercial activity. Ethics is more than just knowing the rules around confidentiality, integrity and objectivity. It's about identifying ethical dilemmas, understanding the implications and behaving appropriately. It includes the role of corporate governance, corporate social responsibility and audit; and their increasing impact in the management of organisations.

Wherever business is conducted the legal and administrative framework underpins commercial activity. With this in mind the areas of contract law, employment law, administration and management of companies is considered.

Assessment strategy

There will be a two hour computer based assessment, comprising 85 compulsory objective test questions.

Syllabus structure

The syllabus comprises the following topics and weightings:

Weight	Syllabus topic
30%	A. Business Ethics and Ethical Conflict
45%	B. Corporate Governance, Controls and Corporate Social Responsibility
15%	C. General Principles of the Legal System, Contract and Employment Law
10%	D. Company Administration

LEARNING OUTCOMES AND INDICATIVE SYLLABUS CONTENT

BA4 – A. BUSINESS ETHICS AND ETHICAL CONFLICT (30%)

Learning outcomes On completion of their studies, students should be able to:			Indicative syllabus content
Lead	**Component**	**Level**	
1 demonstrate an understanding of the importance of ethics to society, business and the professional accountant.	(a) explain the nature of ethics and its application to society, business and the accountancy profession	2	• The importance of ethics. • The nature of ethics and its relevance to society, business and the accountancy profession.
	(b) apply the values and attitudes that provide professional accountants with a commitment to act in the public interest and with social responsibility	3	• Values and attitudes for professional accountants.
	(c) explain the need for a framework of laws, regulations and standards in business and their application and why CIMA and IFAC each have ethical codes	2	• Legal frameworks, regulations and standards for business. • The role of national 'Professional Oversight Boards for Accountancy' and 'Auditing Practices Boards'. • The role of international accounting bodies e.g. IFAC.
	(d) distinguish between detailed rules-based and framework/principles approaches to ethics	2	• Rules-based and framework approaches to ethics.
	(e) identify the ethical issues significant to organisations and how CIMA partners with strategic bodies to assist its members with ethical tensions/synergies	2	• Managing responsible businesses.
	(f) describe how personal and organisational policies and values promote behaviour.	2	• Organisational and personal values.

Learning outcomes On completion of their studies, students should be able to:			Indicative syllabus content
Lead	**Component**	**Level**	
2 explain the need and requirements for CIMA students and members in adopting the highest standards of ethical behaviour.	(a) explain the need to develop the virtues of reliability, responsibility, timeliness, courtesy and respect	2	• The personal qualities of reliability, responsibility, timeliness, courtesy and respect.
	(b) explain the fundamental ethical principles	2	• The fundamental ethical principles, and examples of their use for professional accountants in practice and professional accountants in business. • Continual Professional Development (CPD), personal development and lifelong learning. • Disclosure required by law (confidentiality).
	(c) identify concepts of independence, scepticism, accountability and social responsibility	2	• The concepts of independence, scepticism, accountability and social responsibility.
	(d) illustrate the threats and safeguards to the fundamental ethical principles.	2	• The threats and safeguards approach to resolving ethical issues, including whistle-blowing, grievance, regulations and laws.
3 explain the various means of regulating ethical behaviour, recognising different parties' perspectives towards ethical dilemmas.	(a) explain the relationship between the CIMA Code of Ethics and the law	2	• The relationship between the CIMA Code of Ethics and the law. • The distinction between CIMA's Code of Ethics, contracts, and the responsibilities of students and members when they conflict.
	(b) describe the consequences of ethical behaviour to society, business, the profession and the professional accountant	2	• The consequences of unethical behaviour: reputation, financial, legal and regulatory; and the benefits of good ethical behaviour
	(c) identify conflicting perspectives of interest when dealing with stakeholders in society, business and the values of professional accountants.	2	• The concepts of corporate and personal ethical stances, in relation to multiple stakeholders.

Learning outcomes On completion of their studies, students should be able to:			Indicative syllabus content
Lead	**Component**	**Level**	
4 identify ethical dilemmas and how they may be resolved.	(a) identify situations where ethical dilemmas and conflicts of interest occur, based on CIMA's ethical checklist.	2	• The nature of ethical dilemmas, tensions and synergies. • Conflicts of interest and how they arise. • Issues of corporate confidentiality. • CIMA's Ethical Checklist.

BA4 – B. CORPORATE GOVERNANCE, CONTROLS AND CORPORATE SOCIAL RESPONSIBILITY (45%)

Learning outcomes On completion of their studies, students should be able to:			Indicative syllabus content
Lead	**Component**	**Level**	
1 explain the role of corporate governance in meeting the concerns of society and investors over the management of corporations.	(a) describe corporate governance	2	• The role and key objectives of corporate governance, agency theory. • Objectivity and independence.
	(b) explain the interaction of corporate governance with business ethics and company law	2	• The interaction of corporate governance, ethics and the law.
	(c) explain the purpose, definition of the Organisation for Economic Co-operation and Development (OECD) principles of Corporate Governance	2	• The purpose, definition and status of the OECD Corporate Governance Code.
	(d) describe IFAC's main drivers of sustainable corporate success	2	• IFAC's drivers for sustainable organisational success.
	(e) illustrate CIMA's practical proposals for better corporate governance	2	• CIMA's proposals for better reporting of corporate governance.
	(f) distinguish between detailed rules-based and principles-based approaches to governance.	2	• Rules and principles based approaches to governance.
2 explain the impact of corporate governance on the directors and management structures of corporations.	(a) describe the role of the board and different board structures	2	• The role of the board in establishing corporate governance standards. • Types of board structures and the role of the board as independent, objective, sceptical and resourceful.
	(b) explain the effects of corporate governance on directors' powers and duties	2	• The impact of corporate governance on directors' powers and duties.
	(c) describe the types of policies and procedures that constitute 'best practice'	2	• Policies and procedures for 'best practice' in companies.

Learning outcomes On completion of their studies, students should be able to:			Indicative syllabus content
Lead	**Component**	**Level**	
	(d) describe the respective committees and their roles and responsibilities with regards monitoring and controlling the actions of the Executive.	2	• Audit committee – controls, monitoring and relationships. • Appointments Committee. • Remuneration Committee.
3 explain the role of external and internal audit.	(a) identify the requirements for external audit and the basic processes undertaken	2	• External audit.
	(b) explain the meaning of fair presentation	2	• Fair presentation.
	(c) distinguish between external and internal audit	2	• Distinction between external and internal audit.
	(d) explain the purpose and basic procedures of internal audit; the need for financial controls and the purpose of audit checks and audit trails	2	• Internal audit. • Financial controls, audit checks and audit trails.
	(e) explain the role of internal audit in non-financial monitoring and control activities	2	• The role of internal audit in providing a service to management.
	(f) illustrate the added value internal audit provides to both the board and management of the corporation.	2	• How internal audit plays an important and value added service throughout the corporation both in financial and non- financial processes.
4 explain the nature of errors and frauds.	(a) explain the nature of errors	2	• Errors including those of principle, omission, and commission.
	(b) explain the nature of fraud	2	• Types of fraud.
	(c) describe the different methods of fraud prevention and detection.	2	• Methods for prevention of fraud including levels of authorisation, documentation and staff organisation. • Methods of detection of fraud including spot checks, comparison with external evidence, reconciliations and control accounts.

Learning outcomes On completion of their studies, students should be able to:			Indicative syllabus content
Lead	**Component**	**Level**	
5 explain Corporate Social Responsibility (CSR) – a political and corporate perspective.	(a) describe the OECD general policies	2	• The OECD general policies.
	(b) explain the role of national and international laws and regulations	2	• The role of international frameworks.
	(c) describe conflicting demands of stakeholders	2	• The demands of stakeholders, maximising shareholder return and enhancing the supply chain.
	(d) identify issues with CSR and the supply chain.	2	• Issues within the supply chain.
6 explain the role of CSR within company reporting.	(a) describe the guidelines of reporting CSR within annual reports	2	• Disclosure guidelines and sources of best practice.
	(b) identify synergies and tensions with CSR and brand management.	2	• The link between CSR and a company's brand.

BA4 – C. GENERAL PRINCIPLES OF THE LEGAL SYSTEM, CONTRACT AND EMPLOYMENT LAW (15%)

Learning outcomes On completion of their studies, students should be able to:			Indicative syllabus content
Lead	**Component**	**Level**	
1 explain how the law determines the point at which a contract is formed and the legal status of contractual terms.	(a) identify the essential elements of a valid contract and situations where the law requires the contract to be in a particular form	2	• The essential elements of a valid contract.
	(b) explain how the law determines whether negotiating parties have reached agreement and the role of consideration in making that agreement enforceable	2	• The legal status of statements made by negotiating parties. Offers and acceptances and the application of the rules to standard form contracts using modern forms of communication.
	(c) explain when the parties will be regarded as intending the agreement to be legally binding and how an agreement may be avoided because of misrepresentations	2	• The principles for establishing that the parties intend their agreement to have contractual force and how a contract is affected by a misrepresentation.
	(d) explain how the terms of a contract are established and their status determined	2	• Incorporation of express and implied terms, conditions and warranties.
	(e) explain the ability of a company to contract.	2	• Corporate capacity to contract.
2 explain the essential elements of an employment contract and the remedies available following termination of the contract.	(a) explain how the contents of a contract of employment are established	2	• The express and implied terms of a contract of employment. • The rights and duties of employers and employees.
	(b) explain what policies and procedures may be present in the workplace	2	• Diversity, discrimination, anti-bribery, gifts, conflicts of interest, whistle- blowing, money laundering, disciplinary, data protection, social media, health and safety.
	(c) explain the distinction between unfair and wrongful dismissal and the consequences	2	• Notice and dismissal, redundancy. • Unfair and wrongful dismissal.

BA4 – D. COMPANY ADMINISTRATION (10%)

Learning outcomes On completion of their studies, students should be able to:			Indicative syllabus content
Lead	**Component**	**Level**	
1 explain the nature, legal status and administration of business organisations.	(a) describe the essential characteristics of the different forms of business organisations and the implications of corporate personality	2	• The essential characteristics of sole traders, partnerships, companies limited by shares and corporate personality. • 'Lifting the corporate veil' both at common law and by statute.
	(b) explain the differences between public and private companies	2	• The distinction between public and private companies. • Company registration and the advantages of purchasing a company 'off the shelf'.
	(c) explain the purpose and legal status of the Articles of Association	2	• The purpose and contents of the Articles of Association.
	(d) explain the main advantages and disadvantages of carrying on business through the medium of a company limited by shares.	2	• The advantages and disadvantages of a company limited by shares.

Section 1

OBJECTIVE TEST QUESTIONS

SYLLABUS SECTION A: BUSINESS ETHICS AND ETHICAL CONFLICT

1 Which of these is the most accurate statement of when an accountant should act, having identified a threat to ethical conduct?

A when there is a substantial threat to the profession or their firm?

B when there is a possibility of some professional liability?

C when there is anything other than an insignificant consequence?

2 Ethical frameworks can draw both on rules and on framework principles. Which of the following best expresses the complementary role of ethical rules and principles?

A Ethical rules outline the things you must do and the way you should do them, while framework principles provide guidance on things you ought to do, but leave you to determine how to comply

B Ethical rules provide for conduct that must be complied with in a particular way, while framework principles provide the reasons why standards and rules must be complied with

C Ethical rules provide a clear means to identify what you must do, while framework principles provide the means to identify, evaluate and address ethical problems

3 Which of the following statements are true?

A An accountant is under no duty to disclose the limitations of their expertise to the client

B An accountant is only responsible for his or her own professional qualifications and training

C An accountant may need to compromise the most precise attention to detail in preparing work in order to meet a reasonable deadline

4 Consider the list of safeguards for ethical conduct and choose which are primary workplace (internal) safeguards (A) and which are regulatory (external) safeguards (B).

Try to match internal safeguards to their external counterparts.

1 Appropriate disciplinary processes.

2 Code of Ethics.

3 Continuing professional development requirements.

4 Corporate governance regulations.

5 Educational, training and experience requirements for entry into the profession.

6 Effective, well-publicised complaints systems operated by the employing organisation, the profession or a regulator, which enable colleagues, employers and members of the public to draw attention to unprofessional or unethical behaviour.

7 External review by a legally empowered third party of the reports, returns, communications or information produced by a professional accountant.

8 Leadership that stresses the importance of ethical behaviour and the expectation that employees will act in an ethical manner.

9 Policies and procedures to implement and monitor the quality of employee performance.

10 Professional or regulatory monitoring and disciplinary procedures.

11 Professional standards.

12 Recruitment procedures in the employing organisation emphasising the importance of employing high calibre competent staff.

13 Strong internal controls.

14 The employing organisation's ethics and conduct programmes.

15 The employing organisation's systems of corporate oversight or other oversight structures.

16 Timely communication of the employing organisation's policies and procedures, including any changes to them, to all employees and appropriate training and education on such policies and procedures.

17 Policies and procedures to empower and encourage employees to communicate to senior levels within the employing organisation any ethical issues that concern them without fear of retribution.

18 An explicitly stated duty to report breaches of ethical requirements.

5 Which of these are ethical reasons for the need for continuous improvement and lifelong learning?

A Because they are essential for career progression

B Because qualifications are important so the public can see that accountants are capable

C Because the world of accountancy is constantly developing and it is the accountant's duty to keep up

D Because otherwise there may be costly mistakes made

E Because learning is a good thing in itself

F Because firms are audited for the qualifications of their staff

6 Which of these are explicitly virtues promoted by the CIMA Code of practice?

A Reliability

B Accuracy

C Diversity awareness

D Financial responsibility

E Social responsibility

F Loyalty

G Courtesy

H Fidelity

I Punctuality

J Respect

7 Does an accountant breach his duty of integrity if the accountant:

A Leaves a client to discover important information that is freely available?

B Only tells the client the information they have specifically asked for or that is habitually provided?

C Forgets to mention something important?

D Withholds information that may be compromising for the employer?

8 Which of the following is true?

A It is acceptable to discuss client information with a person who knows nothing about your job or business

B Prospective or past clients are owed a lesser duty of confidentiality than current clients

C Nothing learned as a consequence of working for one client may be used in relation to another

9 Identify the statement that best describes the relationship between CIMA's Code of Ethics and that of IFAC:

A The CIMA Code is a framework, whereas IFAC provides the rules

B The IFAC Code is a framework, whereas the CIMA Code provides the rules

C Both are essentially the same frameworks, but CIMA's Code has been adjusted to meet local regulatory conditions

D The IFAC Code is an important guidance, but you can get disciplined for breaching CIMA's Code

10 Which of the following statements is true?

A The Financial Reporting Council is a government body which regulates the ethics for the profession

B The Professional Oversight Body for Accountancy decides on what changes need to be made to the professional rules and puts new ethical rules into place

C The Auditing Practices Board advises, consults on and sets Ethical Standards for auditors

11 Which of these is not a principle of standards in public life?

A Transparency

B Honesty

C Accountability

12 Corporate responsibility means:

A That the company, not the individual is ultimately responsible for the values of the accounting professionals it employs

B That a company has the responsibility to do what is in the best interests of its clients, employees and shareholders

C That a company has to ensure that it has a charitable and environmentally friendly marketing approach

D That a company reviews and considers the impact of its policies and practices to ensure that plays a positive and contributory role in relation to its stakeholders, the community and the environment

13 What three Rs, together with timeliness and courtesy, constitute the personal qualities one would expect of a professional accountant?

A Regulation, Registration, Remuneration

B Respect, Reliability, Realism

C Reliability, Responsibility, Regulation

D Respect, Responsibility, Reliability

14 When might it be appropriate for an accountant to disclose information, provided in confidence?

A At the request of the client

B At the request of the regulator

C At the request of a solicitor

D At the request of the employer

15 In respect of the following problem situations, would you refer primarily to (A) the IFAC Code, (B) the CIMA Code, (C) the Law, or (D) apply professional judgement:

1 A request to disclose data relating to a client to a non-accounting regulatory body, for example the Inland Revenue

2 A dispute over the proper returns relating to an off-shore company and whether you have an ethical duty to apply a higher level of compliance than is required by the foreign jurisdiction's law

3 Pressure being exerted as a result of a change of government policy on the public sector client you are working for

4 Disclosing information you have in your possession, that has not been actually requested, but might assist an investigation by CIMA into alleged ethical wrongdoing

16 Classify the following (A) to (B), according to the situations below (1 – 5):

A Self-interest threats

B Self-review threats

C Advocacy threats

D Familiarity threats

E Intimidation threats

1 Preparing accounts for a campaign group of which the accountant is a leading member

2 Preparing accounts under an unrealistically imposed deadline by a major client

3 Preparing accounts for your close relative's business

4 Preparing accounts for your spouse's business

5 Preparing accounts and providing a basic audit function on those accounts

17 Which of the following statements are true?

A An accountant will not be in breach of the CIMA Code of Ethics where the accountant has inadvertently compromised an ethical principle, so long as he remedies his mistake as soon as possible, following the appropriate safeguards

B An accountant is not obliged to evaluate threats that might compromise ethical principles if he has no actual knowledge of the problem

C An accountant should consider non-financial circumstances known about a situation, as well as the financial data presented when considering a threat to ethical standards

D An accountant should refuse to work for a client or resign his job if he is unable to apply appropriate ethical safeguards

18 Which of these correctly outlines the process for addressing ethical problems?

A Identify the potential for ethical conflict and avoid it, otherwise seeks guidance from CIMA, a manager or a legal adviser

B Identify the facts, apply the framework, seek an internal resolution, ask CIMA

C Identify any principles involved, follow internal procedures, apply the Code if that does not resolve it and then ask CIMA

D Identify the facts, the issues of ethics, principles of the Code involved, use the internal procedures and if all else fails, ask CIMA

19 Where there is no safeguard provided by professional standards, but an accountant has encountered a threat, should the accountant:

A weigh up the likelihood of harm and cautiously applying good sense? or

B take legal advice before proceeding? or

C avoid the activity altogether?

20 Where an accountant encounters a fraud the disclosure of which would be a breach of professional confidence, should the accountant:

A maintain their duty of confidence?

B disclose the fraud immediately?

C take legal advice or consult CIMA?

21 Under which of these circumstances might it be permissible to disclose client information:

A when the client has asked you to disclose and you are lawfully entitled to do so?

B to help a colleague defend a professional misconduct claim?

C to assist in undertaking a review or audit for professional standards purposes?

D to help provide an accurate budgetary statement for the employer?

E to respond to a solicitor's letter, representing someone suing the client?

Case study Questions 22–26

You are approached by your colleague Sima, who has received a complaint from a client (1) because she has not been able to produce a promised report on time (2). Sima says that this is because there is a new software system that she has not got to grips with yet (3), because she could not make it to the training event (4). Sima would like you to contact the client to tell them that there has been a problem with the system (5). She tells you more than you wish to know (6) about the background to the client's request. Office practice is for this type of report to be checked by a colleague before being sent out. Sima says that she has checked her own report, but asks you to sign it off without looking at it (7). You and Sima are friends and so you want to help (8). She says there is a drink in it for you (9) if you help. She also tells you not to tell anyone in case she gets into trouble (10).

22 Which of the actions in the case study compromise integrity?

23 Which of the actions in the case study compromise objectivity?

24 Which of the actions in the case study compromise professional competence and due care?

25 Which of the actions in the case study compromise confidentiality?

26 Which of the actions in the case study compromise professional behaviour?

27 Your boss approaches you to attend a reception on her behalf to represent the firm to the client. You deal with a competitor firm as your own client. There is nothing you are aware of that makes you think that either firm would have a problem with it, but it makes you a little uneasy. Would you:

A Ignore the problem and do as your boss asks?

B Decline on the basis that you have a (fictional) alternative engagement?

C Accept and not tell the other client on the basis that what they do not know will not hurt them?

D Consider the facts and the likelihood of a conflict of interests somewhere down the line and go if you can see no likely difficulty?

E Ask the other client whether they mind you going?

28 You have failed to make a record of a piece of work on a client's account. It would mean that you would not be able to bill the client for it under the firm's billing procedure. You are pretty sure that you remember sufficient details to put in a realistic guesstimate. Do you:

A enter the guesstimate and get on with another job?

B leave the entry blank, so the firm cannot claim for your time?

C contact the client and explain the situation at the risk of undermining their confidence in the firm?

D tell the boss and wait for the explosion?

29 Which of the following would be of use when trying to find a resolution to a serious ethical breach?

A CIMA

B Board of your organisation

C Audit committee of your organisation

D Legal and Compliance department

E Your solicitors

F Your line-manager

30 What is the most important first step when dealing with a potential ethical problem?

A Tell your boss

B Read the CIMA Code of Practice

C Make a thorough and rapid check of the facts

D Ask a colleague their opinion

31 E, a trainee management accountant, prepares an annual analysis of the performance of all staff, including her own. The analysis is used by the financial director to calculate staff bonuses each year.

According to the CIMA code of ethics for professional accountants which of the threats listed below would apply to E?

A Advocacy threat

B Intimidation threat

C Familiarity threat

D Self-interest threat

32 R, a trainee management accountant is employed by JH. R has prepared the draft annual financial statements for JH and presented them to JH's Chief Executive prior to the executive board meeting. The Chief Executive has told R that the profit reported in the financial statements is too low and must be increased by $500,000 before the financial statements can be approved by the executive board.

Which of the threats listed below would apply to R in this situation, according to the CIMA code of ethics for professional accountants?

A Advocacy threat

B Self-review threat

C Intimidation threat

D Self-interest threat

Data for questions 33 and 34

CX, a professional accountant is facing a dilemma. She is working on the preparation of a long term profit forecast required by the local stock market listing regulations.

At a previous management board meeting, her projections had been criticised by board members as being too pessimistic. She was asked to review her assumptions and increase the profit projections.

She revised her assumptions, but this had only marginally increased the forecast profits.

At yesterday's board meeting the board members had discussed her assumptions and specified new values to be used to prepare a revised forecast. In her view the new values grossly overestimate the forecast profits.

The management board intends to publish the revised forecasts.

33 Which TWO of following ethical principles does CX face?

A Integrity

B Confidentiality

C Professional care and due competence

D Objectivity

E Professional behaviour

34 Place the following options into the highlighted boxes in the table below to correctly show the order CX should deal with an ethical dilemma.

Report internally to immediate management
Report externally
Remove herself from the situation
Gather evidence and document the problem
Report internally to higher management

	Dealing with an ethical dilemma
1	
2	
3	
4	
5	

Data for questions 35 and 36

RS, an employee, prepares monthly management accounting information for XYZ which includes detailed performance data that is used to calculate staff bonuses. Based on information prepared by RS this year's bonuses will be lower than expected.

RS has had approaches from other staff offering various incentives to make accruals for additional revenue and other reversible adjustments, to enable all staff (including RS) to receive increased or higher bonuses.

35 Which TWO of following ethical principles does RS face?

A Integrity

B Confidentiality

C Professional care and due competence

D Objectivity

E Professional behaviour

36 Which of following ethical threats does RS face?

A Advocacy threat

B Self-review threat

C Intimidation threat

D Self-interest threat

37 Which ONE of the following is NOT a fundamental principle of the CIMA Code of Ethics?

A Objectivity

B Integrity

C Confidentiality

D Responsibility

38 Ace is a management accountant working as part of a small team that has been set up by ZY, his employer, to evaluate tenders submitted for contracts being awarded by ZY.

He has just discovered that one of the other team members accepted large payments in exchange for information, from an entity at the time it was considering tendering. Ace suspects that this may have influenced the winning tender submitted by the entity.

Ace should document the situation and then report it internally to his line manager. If this is unsuccessful what should he do next?

A Report it to CIMA

B Report it externally to shareholders

C Report it internally to higher management

D Report it externally to a legal advisor

39 Match the principles from CIMA's Code of Ethics in the list below to the relevant interpretation:

- Confidentiality
- Integrity
- Professional behaviour
- Professional competence and due care
- Objectivity

Principle	*Interpretation*
	Maintaining a relevant level of professional knowledge and skills so that a competent service can be provided.
	Complying with relevant laws and regulations.
	Being straightforward, honest and truthful in all professional and business relationships.
	Not disclosing information unless there is specific permission or a legal or professional duty to do so.
	Not allowing bias, conflict of interest or the influence of other people to override professional judgement.

40 CIMA's Code of Ethics for professional accountants is based upon:

A a framework of fundamental principles

B a framework of strict rules

C a scale of penalties for non-compliance

D sustainability principles and best practice

41 CIMA's Ethical Guidelines require members to:

A act responsibly in the way that all other professionals do

B act responsibly but in a way that satisfies organisational demands and pressures

C act responsibly but in a way that satisfies the individual's own ethical code

D act responsibly, honour any legal contract of employment and conform to employment legislation

42 You are a management accountant working a UK listed chemical company. During the course of your duties, you become aware that the company is dumping waste illegally. You have raised this with your manager who has told you to ignore the issue.

Which of the following is NOT an appropriate course of action to take next?

A Contacting CIMA's ethical helpline for advice

B Reporting the company to the environment agency

C Contacting a journalist at a national newspaper

D Taking the matter to the Audit committee

43 **The CIMA Code of Ethics contains five fundamental principles of professional ethics for management accountants. Which of the following are fundamental principles, according to the Code? (Select ALL correct answers)**

A Confidentiality

B Honesty

C Objectivity

D Respect

E Integrity

44 **Which THREE of the following are valid reasons for disclosing commercially sensitive information to a third party which would NOT breach the ethical principle of confidentiality?**

A It is required due to a professional, ethical dilemma

B It is permitted by law and authorised by the client

C It is required by law

D Failure to disclose could materially disadvantage the third party

E There is a professional duty or right to disclose the information

45 John is a CIMA Member in Practice, and advises a range of individual clients and organisations. John has been asked by a client to write to one of the client's customers, threatening to report them to the tax authorities if they do not pay a debt due to John's client.

To do this would be in breach of which fundamental ethical principle (according to CIMA's Code of Ethics)?

A integrity

B objectivity

C professional competence and due care

D confidentiality

E professional behaviour

46 Graham is a CIMA Member in Practice, and advises a range of individual clients and organisations. Graham has been asked, by his sister, to prepare her tax return. Graham's sister has offered to share any reduction in tax, compared to what she paid last year.

To do this would be in breach of which fundamental ethical principle (according to CIMA's Code of Ethics)?

A integrity

B objectivity

C professional competence and due care

D confidentiality

E professional behaviour

47 Peter is a CIMA Member in Practice, and advises a range of individual clients and organisations. Peter has not carried out any Continuing Professional Development (CPD) activity for five years.

This is in breach of which fundamental ethical principle (according to CIMA's Code of Ethics)?

A integrity

B objectivity

C professional competence and due care

D confidentiality

E professional behaviour

48 Gregor is a CIMA Member in Practice, and advises a range of individual clients and organisations. Gregor has been asked, by a prospective new client, to divulge details of another client's business activities.

To do this would be in breach of which fundamental ethical principle (according to CIMA's Code of Ethics)?

A integrity

B objectivity

C professional competence and due care

D confidentiality

E professional behaviour

49 **CIMA's Code of Ethics recommends a four-step process to resolve any ethical conflict. Identify the correct sequence for those steps.**

Refuse to remain associated with the conflict	
Check the facts	
Escalate externally	
Escalate internally	

50 John is a CIMA member, working as Financial Controller of a listed public company. John has shares in the company, and knows that the share price depends to some extent on the reported profits. John is responsible for producing the published accounts of the company.

According to CIMA's Code of Ethics, which TYPE of ethical threat does this represent?

A self interest

B self review

C advocacy

D intimidation

E familiarity

51 Gemma is a CIMA member, working as Financial Controller of a listed public company.

The company is in the process of applying for additional loan finance. Gemma has been asked to write to the company's bank, providing a forecast of future cash flows which she knows to be very optimistic. .

According to CIMA's Code of Ethics, which TYPE of ethical threat does this represent?

A self interest

B self review

C advocacy

D intimidation

E familiarity

52 Which of the following does not specifically relate to business ethics?

A How a company conducts its relationships with employees and other interested parties such as customers, suppliers and the wider community.

B The standard of behaviour expected of employees and the provision of guidance for those employees.

C The financial viability of the business.

D How a company does business rather than what that business is.

53 Which of the following statement/s is/are correct?

(1) If a person complies with the letter of the law she will always be acting ethically.

(2) Ethics in business is the application of ethical values to business.

(3) If a company has a code of ethics this will eliminate the need for legislation.

A How a company conducts its relationships with employees and other interested parties such as customers, suppliers and the wider community.

B The standard of behaviour expected of employees and the provision of guidance for those employees.

C The financial viability of the business.

D How a company does business rather than what that business is.

54 Which of the following relates to an ethical issue?

A The introduction of new IT systems to ensure the confidentiality of customers.

B The recruitment of a new, highly qualified, finance director.

C The purchase of larger more centrally located business premises to facilitate the expansion of the business.

D The introduction of monthly reporting systems to maximise efficiency.

55 Which of the following statements best describes Relativism?

A Ethical rules may differ depending upon the circumstances and conditions so that, for example, slavery was once acceptable behaviour.

B There is only one set of unchanging universal truths and those truths must always be applied.

C There are certain principles that are always true whatever the consequences.

D Ethics is driven by outcomes and not actions so that if an action achieves a desirable outcome then that action must be ethical.

56 Who suggested that ethical behaviour could be developed by embracing fundamental virtues, such as justice, honesty, and integrity?

A Bentham

B Aristotle

C Kohlberg

D Kant

57 Which of the following statement/s is/ are correct?

(1) CIMA members should behave ethically so as to provide services to the public according to certain standards.

(2) Ethics reflect principles and ideas of behaviour that ought to be adhered to rather than merely conforming to current professional practice.

(3) If an individual believes a course of action is morally wrong this will mean it is also ethically wrong.

A (1) only

B (3) only

C (2) and (3)

D (1) and (2)

58 Which of the following is not a reason for CIMA developing its own ethical code?

A IESBA's Code of Ethics for Professional Accountants was considered to be too stringent.

B CIMA's code reflects its status as a Chartered Institute.

C Its disciplinary code may act as a basis for complaints.

D The code provides steps to identify, explain and problem solve rather than list what can and cannot be done.

Data for questions 59 and 60

XQ, an employee of ABC, prepares monthly management accounting information for ABC. This information includes detailed performance data that is used to evaluate managers' performance. The directors are considering the closure of some facilities and XQ's management information will be included in the review.

XQ has had approaches from a number of concerned managers offering various incentives to make adjustments to the management accounting information to improve their performance statistics.

59 Which THREE of following ethical principles does XQ face?

A Integrity

B Confidentiality

C Professional care and due competence

D Objectivity

E Professional behaviour

F Neutrality

60 XQ should document the situation and report it to whom in the first instance?

A CIMA

B Externally to shareholders

C Internally to an immediate manager

D Externally to a legal advisor

61 IFAC published a code of ethics in 2005. Which of the following statements about IFAC's code is correct?

A All members of professional bodies that are part of IFAC must apply this code.

B IFAC required CIMA to include specific rules in their Code of Ethics.

C IFAC's Code is based on international standards but CIMA's Code is specific to the U.K.

D IFAC issued a Code of Ethics for accountants worldwide as scandals such as Enron and World.com had led to the public losing all confidence in the accounting profession.

62 Which of the following is not considered to be an aim of CIMA's Code of Ethics?

A The Code aims to identify the nature of the personal responsibility that the Management Accountant takes on as part of the price for getting a reasonable salary and status.

B The Code aims to enhance the quality and standards of services provided by accountants.

C The Code aims to provide guidance on how to identify the practical situations where particular care might need to be taken because of the ethical pitfalls involved.

D The Code provides general guidance on how to address the difficult questions raised by ethical pitfalls once they have been identified.

63 Which of the following statements is correct?

A The IESBA (IFAC) Code reflects the standards laid down by CIMA.

B Codes of professional ethics are needed in order to protect the reputation of the profession.

C If a company has a code of ethics it is likely that this will eliminate the need for legislation.

D CIMA has a code of ethics to provide a basis for complaints under CIMA's disciplinary procedures.

64 Which of the following statements are true?

(1) You have been told that one of your colleagues in the accounts department has regularly submitted inflated expenses claims. This is a breach of the fundamental principle of integrity.

(2) You are aware that a colleague in the accounts department regularly takes home reports to check and does so after a few cocktails. This is a breach of the fundamental principle of professional behaviour.

(3) You are employed as Management Accountant and have been asked to dismiss one of your colleagues for misconduct. You are aware that this is untrue and that the Company is trying to reduce the workforce without making the due redundancy payments. This is a breach of the fundamental principle of integrity.

A (1) only

B (2 and (3) only

C (3) only

D (1), (2) and (3)

65 Which of the following fundamental principles of CIMA's Code of Ethics is defined as follows "A professional accountant shall be straightforward and honest in all professional and business relationships"?

A Honesty.

B Professional behaviour

C Due Care

D Integrity

SYLLABUS SECTION B: CORPORATE GOVERNANCE

66 Corporate governance is not concerned with which one of the following?

A Effective control

B Business efficacy

C Fiduciary duties

D Accountability

67 In the scandal involving Enron information relating to which one of the following was withheld in order to maintain confidence in its stocks?

A Corporate losses

B Corporate borrowing

C Director remuneration

D Company reorganisation

68 The aim of corporate governance initiatives is to ensure that entities are run well in the interests of their shareholders and the wider community.

Which of the following does it NOT include?

A The necessity for good internal control

B The necessity for an audit committee

C Relationships with the external auditors

D Relationships with the internal auditors

69 There are different approaches to corporate governance, rules-based and principle-approach.

Place the following options into the highlighted boxes in the table below to correctly show the characteristics of each approach.

Comply with the code or explain why	Applied in the UK
Applied in the US	Penalties for transgression
Instils the code into law	Adhere to the spirit rather than the letter of the code

70 Which two of the following are not a profit-making organisation?

A Partnership

B Local government

C Sole trader

D Limited company

E Charity

71 Which one of the following is not a non-profit-making organisation?

A Public limited company

B Charity

C Clubs

D Central government

72 Which of the following is NOT a key feature of an organisation?

A Controlled performance

B Collective goals

C Social arrangements

D Creation of a product or service

73 Which of the following organisations is normally found in the public sector?

A Schools

B Charities

C Clubs

D Businesses

74 The public sector is normally concerned with:

A making profit from the sale of goods

B providing services to specific groups funded from charitable donations

C the provision of basic government services

75 Which of the following is an organisation which is owned and democratically controlled by the people who buy its goods and services?

A Co-operative

B NGO

C Public sector organisation

D Private sector organisation

76 Which statement best describes the UK stock exchange rules in respect of the UK Corporate Governance Code?

A Both listed and unlisted companies are required to comply with the UK Corporate Governance Code

B Non-compliance with the UK Code will result in a fine

C There is no obligation for companies to comply with the UK Code

D Listed companies must explain any non-compliance with the UK Code

77 Which of the following is not a principle of the OECD framework?

A Disclosure and transparency

B Innovation and adaptability

C Responsibilities of the board

D Shareholders' rights of ownership

78 Which of the following statements are TRUE of a two-tier board?

(1) There is a clear separation between the management and the control of the company

(2) Employee representation results in wider stakeholder involvement

(3) There is an implied involvement of NEDs in the running of the company

A (3) only

B (1) and (3) only

C (1) and (2) only

D (1), (2) and (3)

79 Which of the following statements are NOT requirements of SOX for US companies?

(1) Senior audit partners must be changed every 5 years

(2) Directors may not deal in the shares of their company at any time

(3) If a company's financial statements are restated due to material noncompliance with accounting rules and standards, the CEO and chief finance officer must resign

A (2) only

B (3)

C (2) and (3) only

D (1), (2) and (3)

80 Which of the following is not a responsibility of the nominations (appointments) committee?

A Succession planning for directors

B Managing diversity in the composition of the board

C Preparing a description of the role and capabilities needed for the appointment of the chairman

D Recommendations on the removal and appointment of auditors

81 Which of the following statements explaining Buchanan and Huczynski's definition of an organisation is incorrect?

(1) 'Controlled performance' – an organisation's commitment to operating in a way that is economically, socially and environmentally sustainable. Organisations should ensure this commitment prevails while still upholding the interests of various stakeholder groups.

(2) 'Collective goals' – organisations are defined by their goals. The main goal of a school is to educate pupils. It will therefore be organised differently from a company that aims to make profits.

(3) 'Social arrangements' – someone working alone cannot be classed as an organisation. Organisations are structured to allow people to work together towards a common goal. Usually, the larger the organisation, the more formal its structures.

A (1) only

B (2) only

C (1), (2) and (3)

D (2) and (3) only

82 Not for profit organisations (NFPs) do not see profitability as their main objective. Instead, they seek to satisfy the particular needs of their members or the sectors of society that they have been set up to benefit. Which of the following is not an example of a NFP?

A Partnerships

B H M Revenue and Customs

C Hospitals

D Doctors Without Borders

83 Which of the following are examples of Private Sector organisations?

(1) Non- governmental organisations.

(2) Healthcare for the poor.

(3) Charities.

A (3) only

B (2) only

C (2) and (3) only

D (1) and (3) only

84 Which of the following statements is correct?

A There is some overlap between business ethics, company law and corporate governance. In the event of a conflict the ethical principle should take precedence.

B It is considered wrong and unethical for directors and other insiders to benefit from using insider information to make a profit or avoid a loss.

C Corporate governance is primarily concerned with achieving capital growth for the benefit of shareholders.

D Corporate governance is enforced through the Conduct Committee, a body forming part of the FRC.

85 As a consequence of the failure of which of the following organisations did the US introduce Sarbanes-Oxley legislation to address the many criticisms of reporting and auditing practice?

A Enron

B Maxwell Communications Corporation

C Barings

D Northern Rock

86 Which of the following are reasons why the law needs to be supplemented by an additional body of rules and standards known as Corporate Governance?

(1) The rules of law have not proved watertight and in a number of instances, particularly with regard to Insider Dealing and Bribery, directors have been able to circumvent the law.

(2) Persons and institutions who invest in Public Limited companies usually do so with the aim of achieving good capital growth not because they are interested in how that company is run.

(3) Shares in Public Limited companies are potentially held by thousands of separate investors who are generally united by a common objective other than good returns on their individual investment.

A (1) only

B (3) only

C (1), (2) and (3).

D (1) and (2)

87 Which of the following is not a basic argument for Resource-dependency theory?

A Organisations will have systems and procedures in place to ensure that group goals are achieved.

B Organisations depend on resources which ultimately originate from that organisation's environment.

C An organisation's resources are often in the hands of other organisations.

D Since resources are a basis of power, legally independent organisations can therefore depend on each other.

88 As a result of the Sarbanes-Oxley Act companies are required to report on how they have complied with the Act and, if they have not done so, explain their reasons.

True or False?

89 Which of the following statements does not correctly describe one of the eight drivers of sustainable success published in 2012 by the Professional Accountant in Business?

A Effective leadership and strategy – Deploying effective governance structures and processes with integrated risk management and internal control.

B Financial management – Implementing good practices in areas such as tax and treasury, cost and profitability improvement, and working capital management.

C Operational excellence – Supporting decision making with timely and insightful performance analysis.

D Effective and transparent communication – Preparing high quality business reporting to support stakeholder understanding and decision making.

90 Which of the following statements about The Organisation for Economic Co-operation and Development is correct?

(1) The OECD has prepared a code of practice for all members of the EU to assist member governments in their efforts to improve corporate governance in their respective countries.

(2) The OECD has prepared a set of principles intended to assist the 34 members to improve corporate governance in their respective countries.

(3) The OECD has prepared a paper to support the global accountancy profession listing 8 drivers of sustainable organisational success to help organisations to achieve sustainable value creation.

A (1) only

B (3) only

C (2) only

D None of the above

91 German boards often comprise a supervisory and a management board,; which of the following would not be regarded as the role of the management board?

A Preparing agendas for meetings

B Safeguarding the interests of its stakeholders

C Preparing financial reports for meetings

D Day to day running of the enterprise

92 Boards in many countries operate a unitary structure. Which of the following options contains two countries that generally use this system?

A France and Germany

B UK and Germany

C USA and Germany

D USA and UK

93 Corporate governance of public listed companies was the subject of various reports prepared for the Stock Exchange. Which of the following reports dealt predominantly with director's remuneration and led to the principle that there should be a correlation between salary and performance?

(1) The Turnbull Report in 1999.

(2) The Greenbury report in 1995.

(3) The Hampel report in 1998.

A (1) only

B (2) only

C (3) only

D None of the above

94 In the UK Corporate Governance Code which of the following statements regarding the roles of Chairman and Chief Executive is a recommendation?

A The Chairman and Chief Executive roles should be combined if possible so as to avoid unnecessary duplication of tasks.

B The Chairman should have previously been The Chief Executive of the business.

C The Chairman and Chief Executive roles should ideally not be performed by the same person.

D There must always be a Chief Executive appointed.

95 Which of the following is correct in relation to the UK Corporate Governance Code (The Code)?

A The Code is a set of statutory provisions.

B The Code, if broken, can give rise to civil liability.

C Should the Code be breached a fine will be imposed.

D The Code gives rise to disclosure requirements.

96 Which of the following are recommended by the UK Corporate Governance Code?

(1) The board should appoint one of the independent non-executive directors to be the senior independent director to provide a sounding board for the chairman and to serve as an intermediary for the other directors when necessary.

(2) The board should establish an audit committee of at least 5, or in the case of smaller companies 3, independent non-executive directors.

(3) Except for smaller companies, at least one quarter of the board, excluding the chairman, should comprise non-executive directors determined by the board to be independent.

A (1) only

B (1) and (2) only

C (1) and (3) only

D (1), (2) and (3)

97 What requires public listed companies to comply with the UK Corporate Governance Code?

A The Sarbanes-Oxley Act.

B The Companies Act.

C The Cadbury report.

D The London Stock Exchange.

98 Which of the following statements is not a measure introduced by the Sarbanes-Oxley Act?

A An independent five man board called the Public Company Oversight Board to be established, with responsibilities for enforcing professional standards in accounting and auditing.

B All companies with a listing for their shares in the US must provide a signed certificate to the SEC vouching for the accuracy of their financial statements (signed by CEO and chairman).

C The board should establish formal and transparent arrangements for corporate reporting and risk management and internal control principles and for maintaining an appropriate relationship with the company's auditor.

D Restrictions are placed on the type of non-audit work that can be performed for a company by its firm of auditors.

99 Which of the following statements is perceived as a disadvantage of a governance code?

(1) Management consultancy, McKinseys, found that global investors were willing to pay a significant premium for companies that are well governed.

(2) The impact varies depending on the nature of the company and the global viewpoint.

(3) The process is reactionary rather than proactive, responding to major failures in governance.

A (3) only

B (2) only

C (1) only

D (2) and (3) only

100 Which of the following types of committee is not required by the UK Corporate Governance Code?

A Audit Committee

B Supervisory Committee

C Remuneration Committee

D Nomination/Appointments Committee

SYLLABUS SECTION B: CONTROLS

101 Which TWO of the following is NOT a benefit of an external audit?

A The financial statements will not have any errors in them

B Applications to third parties for finance may be enhanced

C Avoids breaking the law, for some entities an audit is not an option

D It is likely to act as a fraud deterrent

E The auditors will assist in the preparation of the financial statements

102 Below are a number of statements regarding internal and external audit. Which FOUR of the statements relate to internal audit rather than external?

A It is a legal requirement for larger companies

B The scope of work is decided by management

C Can be undertaken by employees of the company

D Ultimately reports to the company's shareholders

E Reviews whether financial statements are true and fair

F Must be undertaken by independent auditors

G Mainly focuses on reviewing internal controls

H Ultimately reports to management

103 The key purpose of internal auditing is to:

A detect errors and fraud

B evaluate the organisation's risk management processes and systems of control

C give confidence as to the truth and fairness of the financial statements

D express an internal opinion on the truth and fairness of the financial statements

104 A is preparing a seminar for the Board of Directors of the company she works for regarding internal and external audit and the differences between the two.

Which TWO of the following points are correct with regards to internal and external audit?

(i) The scope of the internal auditors' work is determined by the management of the company, while external auditors determine the scope of their own work.

(ii) Internal auditors test the organisation's underlying transactions, while external auditors test the operations of the organisation's systems.

(iii) Internal audit and external audit are usually both legal requirements.

(iv) Internal auditors can be employees of the company they audit, while external auditors must not be.

A (i), and (ii) only

B (i) and (iv) only

C (ii) and (iv) only

D (iii) and (iv) only

105 Which of the following statements are correct with regards to external audit?

(i) Due to their in-depth examination of the business, external auditors are often able to provide advice to management on possible improvements to the business.

(ii) External auditors often have an independence problem as they report to management and yet are also expected to give an objective opinion on them.

(iii) External audits can help to resolve management disputes, such as disagreements over company valuations or profit-sharing agreements.

(iv) External auditors have little or no interest in the internal controls of the organisation as these are the responsibility of the internal auditors.

A (i) and (iii)

B (i), (ii) and (iv)

C (i), (iii) and (iv)

D (ii) and (iv)

106 Consider the following two statements:

(1) A comprehensive system of control will eliminate all fraud and error.

(2) Employees working in departments other than Accounts have no responsibility for reporting fraud.

Which of these options is/are correct?

A (1) only

B (2) only

C Both

D Neither

107 A major aim of the internal auditors is to

A reduce the costs of the external auditors by carrying out some of their duties

B report to management on internal controls

C prepare the financial accounts

D report to shareholders on the accuracy of the financial statements

108 Which one of the following is not a necessary part of the stewardship function?

A To maximise profits

B To safeguard assets

C To ensure adequate controls exist to prevent or detect fraud

109 Which of the following statements is correct?

A External auditors report to the directors

B External auditors are appointed by the directors

C External auditors are required to give a report to shareholders

D External auditors correct errors in financial statements

110 The fundamental objective of an external audit of a limited company is to:

A give advice to shareholders

B detect fraud and errors

C measure the performance and financial position of a company

D provide an opinion on the financial statements

111 A 'fair presentation' or 'true and fair view' is one that:

A presents the financial statements in such a way as to exclude errors that would affect the actions of those reading them

B occurs when the financial statements have been audited

C shows the financial statements of an organisation in an understandable format

D shows the assets on the statement of financial position at their fair value

112 Which of the following statements is not correct?

A Internal auditors may review value for money

B Internal auditors should not liaise with external auditors

C Internal audit is part of internal control

D Internal audit should be independent of the activities it audits

113 Many organisations consider outsourcing their Internal Audit function. Which of the following are ADVANTAGES of doing this? (Select ALL correct answers)

A Specialist skills may be more readily available

B Risk of staff turnover is passed to the outsourcing firm

C Better understanding of the organisation's objectives and culture

D May improve independence

E Decisions relating to Internal Audit can be based solely on cost

114 Many organisations consider outsourcing their Internal Audit function. Which of the following are DISADVANTAGES of doing this? (Select ALL correct answers)

A Flexibility and availability may not be as high as with an in-house function

B Decisions relating to Internal Audit may be based solely on cost

C Increased management time

D Possible conflict of interest if provided by the external auditors

E Loss of control over standard of service

115 Internal and external audit have similarities, but several features distinguish between them.

Drag and drop the following distinguishing features into the correct category.

	Internal Audit	**External Audit**
Required by shareholders		
Required by statute		
Reports to Shareholders and Management		
Reports to Audit Committee or Directors		
Reports on financial statements		
Reports on controls		

116 Which of the following best describes the role of the auditor?

A The auditor is responsible for preparing the financial statements on behalf of management

B The auditor is responsible for detecting all fraud

C The auditor tests all balances as part of their audit work

D The auditor provides reasonable assurance that the financial statements are correct

117 Which of the following statements is not correct:

A The auditor has the right to call a general meeting of shareholders

B The auditor has the right to access the accounting records of a company

C The auditor has the right to obtain explanations as necessary for the performance of their duties

D The auditor has the right to speak at a general meeting of shareholders

118 Which of the following statements describe the role of the internal audit function?

(1) Appointment is made by the audit committee

(2) The internal audit team must be independent of the company

(3) The internal audit function reports to the shareholders

A (1) only

B (2) only

C (2) and (3) only

D (1), (2) and (3)

119 Which of the following is not one of the five elements of an assurance engagement?

A Subject matter

B Suitable criteria

C Assurance file

D Written report

120 Which of the following statements is false?

A The auditor will express an opinion as to whether the financial statements show a true and fair view

B The audit opinion will provide reasonable assurance

C An audit may not detect all fraud and error in the financial statements

D None of the above

121 Which of the following is not a benefit of an audit?

A Increased credibility of the financial statements

B Deficiencies in controls may be identified during testing

C Fraud may be detected during the audit

D Sampling is used

122 Which of the following is not a purpose of planning the audit?

A To enable the audit to be performed efficiently and effectively

B To enable the appropriate audit team to be assigned

C To ensure the audit is as profitable as possible

D To ensure that the appropriate opinion will be issued when the audit is complete

123 Which of the following statements regarding fraud is correct?

A The auditor may not detect all material fraud in the financial statements but this won't necessarily mean the auditor has been negligent due to the nature of fraud and the likelihood of concealment

B To enable the appropriate audit team to be assigned

C To ensure the audit is as profitable as possible

D None of the above

124 Which of the following is not a benefit of planning the audit?

A It ensures the audit is performed efficiently and effectively

B It helps identify the resources to be allocated

C It ensures the financial statements will be correct

D It minimises the risk the audit will issue an inappropriate opinion

125 Which of the following statement/s is/are correct?

1 Internal auditors always report directly to shareholders

2 The format of external audit reports is determined by management

A 1 only

B 2 only

C Both 1 and 2

D Neither 1 or 2

SYLLABUS SECTION B: CORPORATE SOCIAL RESPONSIBILITY

126 Which THREE of the following are common arguments FOR organisations adopting a strong approach to corporate social responsibility (CSR)?

A Increased profitability due to short term cost reductions

B Faster strategic decision-making

C Improved reputation with environmentally conscious customers

D Ability to attract higher calibre staff

E Reduced chance of government intervention in the future

127 Which TWO of the following statements regarding Corporate Social Responsibility (CSR), ethics and sustainability are correct?

A To be successful, the ethical tone within the organisation needs to come from senior management

B Sustainability refers to a firm's obligation to maximise its positive impact on stakeholders while minimising the negative effects

C Management accountants have a responsibility to promote an ethical corporate culture

D Sustainability and CSR will lead to cost savings, but only in the long-term

128 H operates a successful bakery. He has recently started recycling all waste generated by his store in response to government legislation. At the request of a local charity, he has also started donating any leftover food at the end of each day to a shelter for the homeless.

According to Carroll, which ONE of the following philosophies best describes H's actions?

A Accommodation

B Proaction

C Reaction

D Defence

129 Which THREE of the following are included within Carroll's four-part model of corporate social responsibility?

A Stakeholder responsibility

B Shareholder responsibility

C Legal responsibility

D Ethical responsibility

E Economic responsibility

130 According to CIMA's report 'Evolution of corporate sustainability practices', there are ten elements of organisational sustainability. These are grouped under three headings.

For each of the following elements, identify which relevant heading they should be included under by placing them in the appropriate box.

Elements:

- Board and senior management commitment
- Champions to promote sustainability and celebrate success
- Extensive and effective sustainability training
- Ensuring sustainability is the responsibility of everyone within the organisation
- Including sustainability targets and objectives in performance appraisal

Place each of the above elements into a box under the appropriate heading below.

Strategy and oversight	Execution and alignment	Performance and reporting

131 Which of the following are matters that are generally regarded as relating to Enlightened Self Interest?

(1) Corporations perceived as ethically sound are rewarded with extra customers.

(2) Employees are more attracted to work for, and are more committed to, socially responsible companies.

(3) Positive contribution to society may be a long term investment in a safer, better educated and more equitable community creating a more stable context in which to do business.

A (1) and (2) only

B (2) and (3) only

C None of the above

D All of the above

132 Which of the following definitions of Corporate Social Responsibility produced by the World Business Council for Sustainable Development (WBCSD) is the correct one?

A CSR is the continuous commitment by business to behave ethically and contribute to economic development while improving the quality of life of the workforce and their families as well as the local community and society at large.

B CSR is about capacity building for sustainable livelihoods. It respects cultural differences and finds the business opportunities in building the skills of employees, the community and the government.

C CSR encompasses the economic, legal, ethical and philanthropic expectations placed on organisations by society at a given point in time.

D CSR should recognise the rights of stakeholders established by law or through mutual agreements and encourage active cooperation between corporations and stakeholders in creating wealth, jobs, and the sustainability of financially sound enterprise.

133 Which of the following is not an example of Carroll's economic model of CSR?

A Shareholders requiring a return on their investments.

B Employees to be provided with safe and fairly paid jobs.

C Sponsor the arts (e.g. Tate & Lyle sponsoring the Tate Gallery in London).

D Customers to be able to obtain good quality products at a fair price.

134 Carroll suggested various strategies that could be employed by a company to respond to social pressure. Which of the following correctly lists these strategies?

(1) Accommodation, communication and commitment.

(2) Reaction, defence, accommodation and pro-action.

(3) targeted growth, capital strategy, and efficiency.

A (1) only

B (2) only

C None of the above

D (3) only

135 Milton Friedman argues that "the business of business is business, its primary purpose is to try and earn a profit". Which of the following statements supports this argument?

A A key part of running a successful business is the ability to offer customers and consumers what they need. One of those needs is often a requirement for socially responsible behaviour from the organisation.

B A socially responsible business will be allowed to operate for longer in society. This will mean that there will be more years of cash flows in the future.

C Acting in a sustainable manner not only helps look after the environment and the wider community, but it strengthens the business and helps ensure its long term survival.

D It is a manager's duty to act in a way that maximises shareholder wealth, while conforming to all relevant laws and customs.

136 The Global Reporting Initiative (GRI) is an international independent organisation that helps businesses, governments and other organisations understand and communicate the impact of business on critical sustainability issues such as climate change, human rights, corruption and many others. GRI has produced The G4 Sustainability Reporting Guidelines. Which of the following is not considered to be an environmental aspect of the guidelines?

A Products and services.

B Transport.

C Procurement practices.

D Materials.

137 Which of the following matters within the social aspects of the G4 guidelines is correct with regard to the sub category of human rights?

(1) Training and education.

(2) Marketing communications.

(3) Equal remuneration.

A (1) and (2) only

B None of the above

C (2) and (3) only

D (3) only

138 The G4 Guidelines sets out Principles for Defining Report Content and Principles for Defining Report Quality. Which of the following definitions is correctly stated below?

A Balance principle: The report should reflect positive and negative aspects of the organisation's performance to enable a reasoned assessment of overall performance.

B Accuracy principle: The organisation should select, compile and report information In a consistent way. The reported information should be presented in a manner that enables stakeholders to analyse changes in the organisation's performance over time, and that could support analysis relative to other organisations.

C Materiality principle: The report should include coverage of material aspects and their boundaries, sufficient to reflect significant economic, environmental and social impacts, and to enable stakeholders to assess the organisation's performance in the reporting period.

D Reliability principle: The organisation should report on a regular schedule so that information is available in time for stakeholders to make informed decisions.

139 A stakeholder is a group or individual, who has an interest in what the organisation does, or an expectation of the organisation. There are three categories; internal, connected and external. Which of the following is an example of an external category of stakeholder?

A Managers/Directors

B Finance providers

C Shareholders

D Government

140 Which of the following stakeholders' needs or expectations are correctly described?

(1) The community at large will not want their lives to be negatively impacted by business decisions.

(2) Employees will want to take an active part in the decision making process.

(3) Shareholders' will want dividends and capital growth and the continuation of the business.

A (1) only

B (1) and (2) only

C (1) and (3) only

D All of the above

141 The OECD Guidelines for Multinational Enterprises (the OECD Guidelines), were adopted in 1976, at a time when there was growing concern about the negative impact of corporate practices, particularly on developing countries. Which of the following statements about The OECD guidelines is incorrect?

A The OECD Guidelines are nonbinding recommendations addressed by governments to multinational enterprises operating in or from adhering countries.

B The OECD Guidelines provide voluntary principles and standards for responsible business conduct in areas such as information disclosure.

C The Guidelines are signed by the 30 OECD participating countries.

D The OECD Guidelines have application to all sectors of business and cover companies operating in or from OECD member states worldwide and addresses their supply chain responsibilities.

142 A company has been colluding with a competitor to fix the price of its goods. According to Carroll's model of CSR, this shows a lack of:

A Economic responsibility

B Ethical responsibility

C Legal responsibility

D Philanthropic responsibility

143 Which country believes that 'CSR is about business giving back to society'?

A Philippines

B Ghana

C Canada

D France

144 Complete the sentence below by placing one of the following options in the space.

Corporations perceived as ethically sound ______________.

tend to have higher costs
sell premium products
are rewarded with extra customers

145 According to Carroll's model of CSR, which is the highest responsibility?

A Economic

B Legal

C Ethical

D Philanthropic

146 Which of the following stakeholder has the expectation to take part in the decision making process?

A Employees

B Managers

C Community

D Trade unions

147 Which of the following is not an area covered by the ILP Tripartite Declaration of Principles Concerning Multinational Enterprises and Social Policy?

A Employment

B Anti-corruption

C Training

D Industrial relations

148 Complete the sentence below by placing one of the following options in the space.

The OECD guidelines for Multinational Enterprises _____________.

provide a mandatory code
provide binding principles
provide voluntary principles

149 The 1992 Rio Declaration Agenda 21 agreement provides guidance for:

A governments

B governments and business

C governments, business and individuals

D governments, business, individuals and charities

150 Which of the following is not covered by the UN Global Compact?

A Human rights

B Labour standards

C Environment

D Competition

SYLLABUS SECTION C: THE LAW OF CONTRACT

151 A display of goods in a shop window will generally constitute:

A An offer

B An invitation to treat

C A statement of intention

152 Acceptance is not effective if through:

A Conduct only

B Express words only

C The offeree's non communicated intention

153 Where the post is a valid means of acceptance, at what point will the offeree have been held to have accepted the offer?

A When the letter of acceptance has been written

B When the letter of acceptance has been correctly addressed, its postage paid, and posted

C When the letter of acceptance is received by the offeror

154 A warranty can be classified as:

A A lesser term in a contract

B The most important term in a contract

C Not a term of a contract at all

155 Which of the following is NOT a type of term?

A Warranty

B Condition

C Representation

156 Breach of which of the following term/s would NOT entitle the innocent party to cancel the contract?

1 Warranty

2 Condition

A 1 only

B 2 only

C Both 1 and 2

157 What are the requirements for a valid and binding contract?

A Offer and acceptance only

B Offer, acceptance and consideration only

C Offer, acceptance, consideration and intention to create legal relations

158 Which of the following statements is correct?

A Executory consideration is consideration that is yet to be provided

B Executory consideration is consideration that has already been provided

C Executory consideration is consideration that is insufficient in the eyes of the law

159 Which of the following is NOT an essential element of a valid contract?

A The contract must be in writing

B The parties must be in agreement

C Each party must provide consideration

160 An agreement to carry out an act which the law requires anyway amounts to:

A Sufficient consideration

B Insufficient consideration

C Past consideration

161 Which of the following is NOT required for revocation of an offer to be effective?

A It must be in writing

B It must be made before the offer is accepted

C It must be made by the offeror or a reliable third party

162 In relation to social and domestic agreements the court:

A Assumes the parties did intend to create a legally binding contract

B Presumes that the parties did not intend to create a legally binding contract

C Does not consider the intention of the parties

163 Which of the following statements correctly describes express terms?

A They are regarded as conditions

B They are always in writing

C They are terms that the parties have specifically agreed

164 The principal effect of a counter-offer is:

A It destroys the original offer and replaces it with a new offer

B It creates a binding contract based on the terms of the counter-offer

C It creates a binding contract based on the terms of the original offer

165 S offers to sell his car to B for £10,000 cash. At what point in time does the contract come into being?

A When B accepts the offer

B When B pays S the £10,000

C When the agreement is written down

D When the agreement is signed

SYLLABUS SECTION C: THE LAW OF EMPLOYMENT

166 Which of the following does NOT constitute a duty owed by an employee towards his employer under the common law?

A A duty not to misuse confidential information

B A duty to provide faithful service

C A duty to obey all orders given to him by his employer

167 Which of the following is NOT valid for the dismissal of an employee?

A Dishonesty

B Wilful disobedience of a lawful order

C Membership of a trade union

168 A summary dismissal occurs when:

A The parties agree to end the contract immediately

B The employer terminates the contract with notice but no investigation

C The employer terminates the contract without notice

169 Where a constructive dismissal has been alleged it is:

A Unnecessary to show that the employer intended to repudiate the contract

B Necessary to show that the employer had a history of forcing employees out of their jobs

C Necessary to show that the employer intended to repudiate the contract

170 Anne works for E plc under a 4-year fixed-term contract of employment. At the end of the 4 years, E plc fails to renew the contract because Anne is pregnant.

Which of the following statements is /are correct?

(i) Anne will succeed in an action against E plc for wrongful dismissal,

(ii) Anne will succeed in an action against E plc for unfair dismissal.

A (i) only

B (ii) only

C Both (i) and (ii)

D Neither (i) nor (ii)

171 Which of the following statements is/are correct?

(i) An employer has an implied duty to behave reasonably and responsibly towards employees,

(ii) An employer has an implied duty to provide a reference.

A (i) only

B (ii) only

C Both (i) and (ii)

D Neither (i) nor (ii)

172 An employee has been informed by their employer that they are legally obliged to obey any lawful and reasonable orders.

Which of the following statements is true?

A This is an example of a contractual term implied by the courts

B This is an example of a contractual term implied by legislation

C This is most likely to be an express contract term

D The employer is incorrect, there is no legal obligation for an employee to obey lawful and reasonable orders

173 An employee resigns due the employer committing a serious breach of their employment contract.

Which of the following remedies is open to the employee?

A Redundancy pay

B No remedy is available to an employee who resigns

C Constructive dismissal

D Statutory sick pay

174 In the context of employment law, which of the following statements is true?

A Terms can only be implied into employment contracts by the courts

B Employees must obey ALL orders given by their employer

C Employees must act with reasonable skill and care in the performance of their duties

D Express contract terms always override implied contract terms

175 In the context of employment law, which of the following is NOT a remedy for unfair dismissal?

A Re-instatement

B Re-engagement

C Monetary compensation

D A favourable employment reference

176 In the context of employment law, there are circumstances where dismissal without notice is NOT 'wrongful'.

In which of the following circumstances does this apply?

(1) Both parties have mutually agreed to terminate the contract without notice

(2) The employee has received payment in lieu of notice

(3) The employee has committed a serious breach of contract

A (1) and (2) only

B (2) and (3) only

C (3) only

D (1), (2) and (3)

177 What are the phases of money laundering?

1 Integration

2 Layering

3 Adjustment

4 Placement

A 1, 2 and 3

B 1 and 2 only

C 2 and 3 only

D 1, 2 and 4

178 Which of the following is a corporate bribery offence?

A Bribing an individual

B Receiving a bribe

C Bribing a public foreign official

D Failure to prevent bribery

179 Which of the following criteria does a person not always have to show in order to receive the protection offered by statute in a case of whistleblowing?

A That the disclosure is a qualifying disclosure

B That it is made with a reasonable belief in its truth

C That he has some documentary evidence of the matter complained of

D That it is made to an appropriate person

180 A disclosure made in respect of one of the following matters would not be a qualifying disclosure. Which one?

A That a criminal offence has been committed

B That his employer has breached a contract

C That the work of his employer is causing damage to the environment

D That his employer is engaging in unsafe working practices

SYLLABUS SECTION D : COMPANY ADMINISTRATION

181 The articles of association of a company forms a contract between:

A The shareholders and the directors in all respects

B The shareholders and the company in all respects

C The shareholders and the company in respect of shareholder rights only

182 Which of the following does NOT need to be submitted when registering a private company limited by shares?

A Details of what the company does

B The name of the company

C The type of company

183 Which of the following is NOT an example of a business organisation?

A A sole trader

B An employee

C A limited company

184 Which of the following is NOT a feature of a general/ordinary partnership?

A The partners have unlimited liability

B The partners have joint liability

C Only up to 20 partners are allowed

185 Which of the following is NOT a feature of a limited company?

A Directors can never be liable for the debts of the company

B The shareholders have limited liability

C The company has a separate legal personality

186 Karishma owns a newsagent, runs it as the manager and employs Tessa as part-time help during the week. Karishma is fully liable for the business' debts. What type of business does Karishma own?

A A partnership

B A company limited by shares

C A sole trader

187 To establish a general/ordinary partnership:

A The partners obtain permission through company law

B The partners obtain permission from Companies House

C The partners simply agree to form the partnership

188 Which of the following statements is/are correct?

(i) The partners in an ordinary partnership jointly own the firm's assets

(ii) The shareholders in a company jointly own the company's assets

A (i) only

B (ii) only

C Both (i) and (ii)

D Neither (i) nor (ii)

189 The Articles of Association of ABC Ltd provide that all disputes between ABC Ltd and its directors must be referred to arbitration. Del is a director of ABC Ltd and is in dispute with the company about late payment of his director's fees.

Which of the following is/are correct?

(i) Del is obliged by the Articles of Association to refer the dispute to arbitration whether or not he is a shareholder.

(ii) Del is obliged by the Articles of Association to refer the dispute to arbitration only if he is a shareholder.

A (i) only

B (ii) only

C Both (i) and (ii)

D Neither (i) nor (ii)

190 Which of the following are NOT bound to one another by the articles of association?

A The company to third parties

B Members to the company

C The company to members

D The company to directors

191 In company law, what is meant by the term 'veil of incorporation'?

A A company is a separate legal entity to its shareholders and directors.

B A company has perpetual succession.

C A company pays corporation tax

D A company owns its own property

192 A company is a separate legal entity to its shareholders and directors.

Which of the following are consequences of separate legal entity?

(1) A company is fully liable for its own debts

(2) A company owns its own property

(3) A company enters into contracts in its own name

A (1) and (2) only

B (1) and (3) only

C (2) and (3) only

D (1), (2) and (3)

193 There are a number of important legal differences between unincorporated businesses (e.g. partnerships), and incorporated businesses (e.g. companies).

Which of the following are characteristics of a COMPANY?

(1) A company has perpetual succession

(2) There is no separation of ownership and management in a company.

A (1) only

B (2) only

C Both (1) and (2) only

D Neither (1) or (2)

194 Complete the sentence below by placing one of the following options in the space.

A sole trader is _________________.

appropriate for large businesses
Inappropriate for large businesses

195 Which of the following does not have perpetual succession?

A General partnership

B LLP

C Company

196 Which of the following is not a difference between a private company and a public company?

A The number of directors

B The requirement for an audit

C The required share capital

D The company's turnover

197 Which of the following is not an advantage of a company limited by shares?

A The members have limited liability

B The company can be dissolved easily

C The company has perpetual succession

D The company is a separate legal entity

198 Complete the sentence below by placing one of the following options in the space.

A partnership agreement _________________.

is available in the public domain
is private to the partners

199 Which of the following is not an area covered by the Articles of Association?

A Appointment of directors

B Directors meetings

C Directors remuneration

D Directors powers

200 Complete the sentence below by placing one of the following options in the space.

The Articles of Association________________.

regulate the relationship between the company and its shareholders
regulate the relationship between the shareholders and its directors
regulate the relationship between the company and its directors
regulate the relationship between the company, its shareholders and its directors

Section 2

ANSWERS TO OBJECTIVE TEST QUESTIONS

SYLLABUS SECTION A: BUSINESS ETHICS AND ETHICAL CONFLICT

1 C

100.2 of the CIMA Code of Ethics requires that 'Professional accountants are required to apply this conceptual framework to identify threats to compliance with the fundamental principles, to evaluate their significance and, if such threats are other than clearly insignificant to apply safeguards to eliminate them or reduce them to an acceptable level such that compliance with the fundamental principles is not compromised.' This is because the highest possible professional standards are expected and the safeguards provide practical and straightforward means by which most ethical problems can be easily addressed.

2 C

100.5 of the CIMA Code of Ethics explain that 'a framework to assist a professional accountant to identify, evaluate and respond to threats to compliance with the fundamental principles.' Rules tend to provide a means of identifying what should or should not be done, but provide little guidance on how to engage in ethical reasoning or problem-solving. You have either broken or not broken a rule, but life is seldom that clear-cut and rules cannot provide for every eventuality.

3 A

False: 130.6 of the Code of Ethics states that 'where appropriate, a professional accountant should make clients, employers or other users of the professional services aware of limitations inherent in the services to avoid the misinterpretation of an expression of opinion as an assertion of fact'.

B

False: 130.5 of the Code of Ethics states that 'a professional accountant should take steps to ensure that those working under the professional accountant's authority in a professional capacity have appropriate training and supervision'.

C

True: 130.4 of the Code of Ethics state that 'diligence encompasses the responsibility to act in accordance with the requirements of an assignment, carefully, thoroughly and on a timely basis'. Inevitably, diligence represents a balance between punctiliousness and punctuality!

4

Safeguards in the work environment include, but are not restricted to:	**Safeguards created by the profession, legislation or regulation include, but are not restricted to:**
The employing organisation's systems of corporate oversight or other oversight structures.	Corporate governance regulations.
The employing organisation's ethics and conduct programmes.	Code of Ethics.
Recruitment procedures in the employing organisation, emphasising the importance of employing high calibre competent staff.	Educational, training and experience requirements for entry into the profession.
Strong internal controls.	External review by a legally empowered third party of the reports, returns, communications or information produced by a professional accountant.
Appropriate disciplinary processes.	Professional or regulatory monitoring and disciplinary procedures.
Leadership that stresses the importance of ethical behaviour and the expectation that employees will act in an ethical manner.	Continuing professional development requirements.
Policies and procedures to implement and monitor the quality of employee performance.	Professional standards.
Timely communication of the employing organisation's policies and procedures, including any changes to them, to all employees and appropriate training and education on such policies and procedures.	Effective, well-publicised complaints systems operated by the employing organisation, the profession or a regulator, which enable colleagues, employers and members of the public to draw attention to unprofessional or unethical behaviour.
Policies and procedures to empower and encourage employees to communicate to senior levels within the employing organisation any ethical issues that:	An explicitly stated duty to report breaches of ethical requirements.

5 A

Is not really an ethical reason. Qualifications are important for career progression, partly because they do mark competence, but self-promotion is not an object of ethical behaviour, but a benefit of it.

B

is relevant, but not really in strict ethical terms. Qualifications do help with public confidence, but the ethical duty of accountants is to be forthright about their own abilities. You may pass an exam, but it does not mean that you really understand something in depth. The duty is to really understand your work and to continue to be better at it, rather than merely to have the piece of paper.

C

is highly relevant because the self-imposed obligation to develop is the only way in which CIMA can ensure that accounting standards are actually met in the current context. The problem that professional bodies face is that it takes longer to put in place new standards and training than is desirable. The accountant is under a continuing duty to actively look for ways in which to provide service that is appropriate to the needs of contemporary business and practice. This is as true of ethical standards as of accounting practice standards.

D

is relevant because causing financial loss to the client or to society is the antithesis of what accountants might wish to do. However, the financial impact of ethical behaviour is not the only consideration. Accountants need to be up to date in areas relating to professional conduct and practice that may not have an obvious or direct effect on financial transactions. The Code makes this quite clear.

E

is a laudable sentiment, but self-development is not actually the ethical motivation for the duty to improve and learn. The duty is to learn and improve in the interests of clients and society.

F

is indirectly relevant. Firms are under an ethical duty to make clear their capabilities and capabilities of their staff. Training and qualification frameworks are essential safeguards for ethical practice. However, the individuals responsibility to develop himself or herself is not because the boss wants to vaunt your qualifications, but because you should be and be seen to be competent to do your job in prevailing professional conditions.

6 A

Reliability is a specific virtue because of the importance of being diligent to the client in the delivery or service, to the profession in the maintenance of a positive reputation and to the public in the trust that can be placed in accountants' reports and assurances.

B

Accuracy is not explicitly stated as a virtue. Accuracy is obviously the product of diligent work and an essential quality in work, but is an outcome, rather than an attribute of a person. Ethical virtues are qualities of people, rather than of work.

C

Diversity awareness is not explicitly addressed by the Code. There are substantial legal duties on people to avoid discrimination in all aspects of life, but accountants are to behave objectively. The general duty of respect for all clients and so on covers respect, regardless of race, gender and so on.

D

Financial responsibility is not a specific object of the Code, since the ethical Code focuses on those circumstances that surround the preparation of work that might affect the reliability or weight of that work.

E

Social responsibility is at the heart of the Code because the accountant owes a duty to the public and society to ensure that financial matters are carried out in an honest and transparent way. In many respects, the development of modern accounting is driven by the need of society to faith in financial processes. Therefore, the accountant should be able to respond (be responsible) to that need.

F

Loyalty, while being a desirable quality in many ways, even reflected in duties of trust and confidence to the employer at law and to clients in terms of confidentiality is not explicitly a part of the Code. Loyalty may, in fact, give rise to ethical problems where loyalty to friends, colleagues, causes or family can conflict with social responsibility. Effectively, the accountant's ultimate responsibility is to the society.

G

Courtesy is specifically mentioned because it links in with respect and professionalism in dealing with clients. While it may seem less critical than some of the other virtues, clearly it is the springboard of other professional relationships, particularly trust, which is the underpinning principle upon which an accountant must base much of his or her work.

H

Fidelity or faithfulness is much the same as loyalty. While it might be generally socially desirable, the professional obligation to society can often mean that duties of fidelity are in conflict with broader public duties.

I

Punctuality is not explicitly said in those words. However, timeliness is. Different words can mean the same thing and the key to the Code is to understand the reasoning, rather than applying the strict letter of the 'law'. Timeliness is vitally important because it is linked to reliability, due diligence and care. No accountant needs reminding that time is money.

J

Respect is a key feature of the Code and underpins the trust needed to maintain professional relationships. If mutual respect is built up, it often makes addressing ethical problems considerably easier and avoids them altogether. It also has an impact on the perception of the profession by the public and the extent to which a firm can be seen to be complying with other social responsibilities like appreciating and responding to the diverse needs of clients.

7

All of these are potentially breaches of the principle of integrity. Even if information is freely available, it may not be clear that it is important in the context of the work undertaken. As such, the accountant may be misleading the client by leaving it to the client to find out something. Similarly, partial information may be highly misleading. Forgetting to mention important information, unless inadvertent, could be classed as being reckless. There is a duty to be careful that is bound up with the concept of integrity. Regardless of the duty of trust and confidence, the client should not be kept in the dark to avoid embarrassment. It may be in the latter circumstances, that some urgent consultations within the firm or with a regulator or legal advisers may be appropriate.

8 A

False: The duty of confidentiality extends even to social situations (140.2 of the CIMA Code).

B

False: The duty of confidence subsists for past, present and future clients (140.3 and 140.6 of the CIMA Code).

C

False: Know-how and skills learned from doing a task is transferable. What is not acceptable is passing on or using information, rather than learning from experience (140.6 of the CIMA Code).

9 C

is probably the most accurate statement, since the CIMA Code draws very heavily from the IFAC Code. There is an element of truth in D as well, since some aspects of the IFAC Code probably set the standards at a lesser level than UK Law and standards would accept. Neither of the first two statements are true. The approach used in both Codes is essentially the same.

10 C

is the correct answer. The Financial Reporting Council is an independent, non-governmental regulator which ensures that corporate bodies in general inspire public confidence because of sound financial reporting, but that it is independent from political interference. The Professional Oversight Body for Accounting can make recommendations for change, but cannot make new rules on its own account.

11 A

is not a Principle of Standards in Public Life. Transparency is important, but it is a quality of processes, not of individuals. The standards focus on the individual's own duty to make systems transparent.

Selflessness and Integrity highlight that self-interest and the vulnerability to outside influences should be avoided. Objectivity and Accountability emphasise the importance of decision-making based on facts and relevant considerations which can be justified with reference to clear reasoning and evidence.

Openness, Honesty and Leadership all are behaviours that require the individual to take on responsibility for what they do and they know and to actively follow the right course of action, engendering trust and confidence.

12 D

is correct. Corporate responsibility is not a question of alleviating the individual responsibility of professionals to act in a professional way, although a company should support, supervise and scrutinise the behaviour of its professional employees and bear responsibility when they fall short of the standards expected of them.

Neither does corporate responsibility mean that traditional business partners, in the sense of employees, clients and stakeholders are the only concern of a business. Nor should good Public Relations (PR) be confused with a sense of responsibility to the community. In many ways, Ethical Values and Corporate Responsibility Agendas will make for good PR, but that is not the motivating factor, nor should it be. Initiatives motivated by marketing, rather than principle are ultimately more likely to inspire cynicism than trust.

13 D

is correct. These are the three aspects that are personal, that is they are part of the behaviour and make-up of an individual, and they are qualities, states of mind or personal attributes, rather than attitudes.

14 B

is correct. Although a client might request the disclosure of information, there may be certain circumstances when that information might include other confidential information, relating to another party. However, when refusing to disclose, reasons should be given and a second opinion in principle might be sought from the person responsible for Information and Data compliance in your organisations. Requests from the regulator, unless they are acting unlawfully, will normally be appropriate to disclose information.

Requests made by solicitors, are not in themselves, requests where there is a legal obligation to disclose. The reason for the request should be a reason where there is a legal or professional obligation to disclose or where the person requesting the information through the solicitor is the sole subject of it. Solicitors' letters should be dealt with in a courteous and timely way, but should not be assumed to have any greater weight in themselves than a request by any other member of the public.

Requests by your employer, other than as part of regulatory review or because the matter is being dealt with by a variety of people across the office, all subject to the same confidentiality, should be treated with care and should fall in the category of acceptable disclosures within the terms of your Data and Information Management procedures. Most damaging breaches of confidentiality occur as a result of internal disclosure where the recipient is unaware of the confidential nature of the material they are receiving.

15

While there is considerable overlap, the following may be your first port of call in resolving the issues raised. In respect of the following problem situations, you would refer primarily to (A) the IFAC Code, (B) the CIMA Code, (C) the Law, (D) or apply professional judgement:

1 **C –** A request to disclose data relating to a client to a non-accounting regulatory body, for example the Inland Revenue, probably raises the question of whether there is a specific legal duty to disclose. If the law requires you to assist a body such as the Inland Revenue, this overrides other obligations. Should you be unclear, you should consult CIMA for advice.

2 **A –** A dispute over the proper returns relating to an off-shore company, if those relate to practices and activities in that jurisdiction would certainly be looked at in the light of the IFAC Code as a minimum. It may be that you feel that a higher level of ethical conduct is the responsible and professional course of action. Work undertaken in relation to the UK, even extra-territorially, should always be done with reference to the applicable domestic law and practice.

3 **D –** Pressure being exerted as a result of a change of government policy on a the public sector client you are working for falls within both the Codes, but primarily is an issue of independence and integrity. Just because a client is operating public policy does not mean that specific actions might be in the public interest.

Examples such as local authority interest rate swaps in the 1980s and 1990s demonstrate that professional vigilance against public pressures as well as private interests are needed. However, this is largely a question of professional judgement.

4 **B –** Disclosing information you have in your possession, that has not been actually requested, but might assist an investigation by CIMA into alleged ethical wrongdoing falls directly within the CIMA Code obligations.

16

A 4 Preparing accounts for your spouse's business will clearly cause a personal conflict of interests.

B 5 In this situation the accountant would be reviewing, as auditor, the work that they had themselves completed which would hinder their independence.

C 1 Being a member of the campaign group, the accountant will be seen to be advocating the group.

D 3 Preparing accounts for someone that you are very familiar with can put pressure on the accountant to act favourably towards, in this situation, their relative.

E 2 Not wanting to lose their major client, the accountant may feel intimidated into meeting the deadline at the cost of the accuracy of their work.

17 A

True: 100.8 of the Code of Practice means that applying safeguards and remedying the problem is the core concern. It is easy to stray into the tricky ethical situations without noticing it. Ethical standards are about taking responsibility for choices, not punishing accountants who are the victims of circumstances.

B

False: 100.6 of the Code of Practice makes it clear that the accountant is responsible not only for what they know, but for what they can reasonably be expected to know. Inadvertent mistakes, by their nature, cannot be avoided. Problems that should be obvious to a well-trained, diligent accountant are their responsibility. 'I did not know' is no excuse if it would have been evident to any accountant.

C

True: 100.7 of the Code of Practice makes it clear that qualitative information should be taken into account. Sometimes the threats to ethics do not arise from accounting itself, but by surrounding circumstances.

D

True: 100.7 of the Code of Practice is pretty explicit about this. Obviously, an employer should have systems in place to allow people to apply safeguards in most situations and to maintain professional ethics. However, it is better to be unemployed than serving a prison sentence!

18 CLEARLY (D) IS THE RIGHT ANSWER.

You need to know what is happening first and work out whether there is an ethical issue arising. You then need to work out what sort of issue it is so you can use the guidance to determine how it ought to be dealt with according to professional standards. If internal mechanisms allow you to resolve it in accordance with professional standards, that is fine, but if there is a conflict between internal practice and the Code, then you may need to look for outside guidance. CIMA's ethics helpline would be a good start.

19 C

100.3 of the CIMA Code of Ethics 'provides examples of safeguards that may be appropriate to address threats to compliance with the fundamental principles and also provides examples of situations where safeguards are not available to address the threats and consequently the activity or relationship creating the threats should be avoided'. Because most frequent problems are anticipated by the Code and because it is drawn up in terms of values and principles, as well as specific rules, it is unlikely that there would be a threat not addressed in some way. However, accountants should not risk ethical misconduct, especially when dealing with new systems and business practices. Remember also that things can be lawful without being ethical!

20 C

The CIMA Code of Practice advises that (c) is the appropriate course of action: '100.20 If a significant conflict cannot be resolved, a professional accountant may wish to obtain professional advice from the relevant professional body or legal advisors, and thereby obtain guidance on ethical issues without breaching confidentiality'.

21 A

True: 140.7 permits this (obviously where there are no other conflicting obligations).

B

True: 140.7 would suggest that this would be appropriate.

C

True: 140.7 requires compliance with technical, quality and regulatory obligations.

D

False: Unless there is a specific regulatory or professional duty, internal budgetary preparations would not, of themselves, justify disclosure.

E

False: A request from a solicitor does not necessarily amount to a legal or regulatory duty to disclose. Solicitors will sometimes ask for things that you could legally disclose, but where it would be not consistent with professional ethics to disclose.

22 **Integrity** – When you are asked to contact the client to tell them that there has been a problem with the system, (5) you are, in effect, being asked to tell a lie. At the very least you would be being reckless with the truth of having checked it if you sign it off without looking at it (7).

23 **Objectivity** – It may be a small inducement, but it is an inducement when Sima says there is a drink in it for you if you help (9). The fact that you and Sima are friends and so you want to help (8) might indicate that you are being influenced in your decision- making by familiarity.

24 **Professional Competence and Due Care** – When Sima says she has not been able to produce a promised report on time (2), it is clear that she is not professionally competent, which is reinforced by the fact that she is not able to operate the new software system that she has not got to grips with yet (3).

25 **Confidentiality** – Generally, you should not be party to more than you wish to know about the background to the client's request (6), but then there can be a duty to disclose to a regulatory body when she tells you not to tell anyone in case she gets into trouble (10).

26 **Professional Behaviour** – There is normally an appropriate way in which a complaint from a client (1) should be dealt with, while there is a continuing duty to develop, not only core skills, but those needed to work effectively for clients. Sima has compromised this when she could not make it to the training event (4).

27 The problem presents potential for a conflict of interest and a simple ethical dilemma.

A

Do you do what your boss wants, or do what is demanded by professional ethics. This is easily solved. Pleasing the boss is lower down the hierarchy of priorities and is not really part of the framework of accounting professional ethics.

B

A lot of people would resolve this in practice by a 'white lie'. The only thing is that you are not actually dealing with the problem and hardly in the spirit of openness and honesty. Besides, although you have not attended, it concedes that your barriers to ethical conduct are your personal convenience, rather than facing up to problems and resolving them.

C

Accepting the invitation may not be a problem if you have already weighed up the facts and decided there is no real potential for conflicting interests, but going and not giving the other client some indication of your intentions so to do may create more problems than it solves. Secrecy, which is the opposite of openness, tends to fuel suspicions;

D

Is the correct answer. Looking at the facts and determining first whether there is an ethical issue is the necessary first step. After that, if there is potential for a conflict of interest, then you should say so to the boss and refuse. If the boss insists, then you might wish to try and resolve it using a third party in the firm. If there is no potential for conflict, it may nonetheless be advisable to check with both clients that they have no objection to ensure that they do not perceive there to be a conflict.

E

Displacing the problem by getting the client to make the decision for you is not managing the problem. Moreover, it may be in one client's perceived interest for you to attend. Conflicts of interest tend to favour one party practically more than the other.

28 A

Generally speaking a guess is a falsification and this is dishonest.

B

Ignoring the problem simply short-changes your employer, which is depriving the employer of fees to which they would have been entitled, had you done your job properly.

C

Maintaining the trust of the client in the firm and the profession is important and, although at some point it may be necessary to inform the client, if you plan to bill them after all, then it is most appropriate for you to use the internal processes first.

D

Unfortunately, we have to face the consequences of our mistakes. There is almost certainly a procedure in the company either for writing off these errors or for communicating and negotiating with clients. However, if your boss simply tells you to falsify it, then this does not absolve you of your ethical responsibility to do the right thing. You may wish to seek alternative advice from another manager or from your audit committee.

29 A

CIMA is always a useful source of advice and guidance, although using your internal processes first may give you a specific local resolution.

B

Board of your Organisation can provide guidance and will ultimately have to take responsibility for the wrongdoings of employees.

C

Audit Committee of your Organisation are there to ensure that care and standards are met. Normally the audit committee will comprise people with considerable experience and expertise in dealing with problems in an effective and professional way.

D

Legal and Compliance Department will often be a good port of call, although there may be a tendency to look at what the rules require, rather than what is ethical best practice.

E

Your solicitors are your affair. If you are worried about your own status, then taking legal advice is sensible, but it would be inappropriate to seek professional guidance on an ethics matter from them.

F

Your line-manager is normally the first port of call, unless he is part of the problem. While a manager cannot relieve you of your personal professional responsibilities for ethical decision-making, they may be able to help shoulder the burden or help you see the problem in a less alarming light.

30 A

Your line-manager is normally the first port of call, unless he is part of the problem. While a manager cannot relieve you of your personal professional responsibilities for ethical decision-making, they may be able to help shoulder the burden or help you see the problem in a less alarming light. However, you need to be aware of all of the facts first.

B

It is assumed that you have read, learned and inwardly digested the CIMA Code of Practice, although revisiting it to check that what you consider is an issue, actually is an ethical problem after you have . . .

C

. . . properly checked your facts. Careful analysis of what is really going on will often reveal that the ethical problem is less difficult than it seems. People often panic when faced with ethical problems and often they will disguise as a dilemma a situation where this only one right course of action, but is simply quite unpalatable. Most 'ethical dilemmas' are confused priorities, e.g. do I please the boss or look after the client's best interests. Most potential conflicts of interests are when there is a really tempting opportunity and you want to have your cake and eat it. Most ethical mistakes cause real problems because people try to hide their mistake and try to undo things for themselves, rather than owning up and seeking help.

D

Most people struggle with ethical problems. Often the people who have been around the longest with the quick 'pragmatic' solution are not actually thinking about the problem at all. Take advice, but always check your facts, check to see whether what you have in front of you is a real ethical issue, seek guidance from the Code and the firm's procedure and use the mechanisms in place in the firm and beyond to face the problem and resolve it.

31 D

E stands to make a gain if he manipulates the figures to get a better bonus, hence E is in a position of a self-interest threat.

32 C

33 A and D

According to CIMA's Code of ethics for professional accountants CX is in a position where she may be compromising her integrity and objectivity.

Integrity – This principle imposes an obligation to be truthful and honest on the accountant. A professional accountant should not be associated with reports or other information where she/he believes that the information contains misleading statements. This seems to be the case with the revised forecasts; CX believes that the revised forecasts are 'grossly overstated'.

Objectivity – A professional accountant should not allow conflict of interest or undue influence of others to override professional or business judgements or to compromise their professional judgements. The management board are overriding CX's professional and business judgement as they are imposing their assumptions on the forecast profits.

34

	Dealing with an ethical dilemma
1	Gather evidence and document the problem
2	Report internally to immediate management
3	Report internally to higher management
4	Report externally
5	Remove herself from the situation

35 A and D

RS must also comply with the CIMA codes fundamental principles of integrity and objectivity. Changing the management information would breach both of these principles.

36 D

37 D

38 C

He should start by gathering all relevant information so that he can be sure of the facts and decide if there really is an ethical problem. All steps taken should be fully documented.

Initially he should raise his concern internally, possibly with the team's manager or a trusted colleague.

If this is not a realistic option, for example because of the relationship of the manager and the team member that Ace is concerned about, he may have to consider escalating the issue and speak to the manager's boss, a board member or a non-executive director. If there is an internal whistle blowing procedure or internal grievance procedure he should use that.

If after raising the matter internally nothing is done and he still has concerns he should take it further, for example if the other team member is an accountant Ace could consider reporting the team member to his professional body.

Ace could also distance himself from the problem and ask to be moved to a different department or to a different team.

39

Principle	*Interpretation*
Professional competence and due care	Maintaining a relevant level of professional knowledge and skills so that a competent service can be provided.
Professional behaviour	Complying with relevant laws and regulations.
Integrity	Being straightforward, honest and truthful in all professional and business relationships.
Confidentiality	Not disclosing information unless there is specific permission or a legal or professional duty to do so.
Objectivity	Not allowing bias, conflict of interest or the influence of other people to override professional judgement.

40 A

The CIMA code of ethics is an example of a principles-based approach as opposed to a rules-based approach.

41 D

42 C

The basic principle here is that of confidentiality. To go outside of the business and professional environment in this manner without first considering the other options presented would not be following recommended process.

A – CIMA's ethics helpline exists to give members advice and is not a breach of confidentiality as it is within the professional arena. B – Reporting the company to the environment agency would comply with relevant legislation, however you would need to sure of your facts before whistle blowing. D – The Audit committee should be all NEDs and therefore a logical place to go, particularly as they are also responsible for the whistle blowing policy.

43 A, C, E

44 B, C, E

These are the three major reasons for disclosure of confidential information to third parties.

45 A

Integrity would be compromised as finance professionals should be straightforward and honest.

46 B

Objectivity would be compromised due to the conflict of interest this situation presents.

47 C

CPD is needed to maintain professional competence.

48 D

Divulging the details requested would breach confidentiality.

49

Refuse to remain associated with the conflict	4
Check the facts	1
Escalate externally	3
Escalate internally	2

50 A

John can ultimately benefit financially from his actions so his objectivity may be compromised.

51 C

Gemma is being asked to promote a position or opinion to the point that subsequent objectivity may be compromised.

52 C

A, B and D options are related to ethics; purely financial matters are not generally an ethically related matter. Ethics are principles that guide behaviour not for decision making on grounds of profit and success. A consequence of unethical behaviour could be lost profits or loss of financial viability.

53 C

The law must always be obeyed but just obeying the law does not necessarily mean those actions are ethical. As a consequence of unethical behaviour the public could lose trust in the accounting profession but simply having a code of ethics will not eliminate the need for legislation; the code must be followed.

54 A

B, C and D options are examples of good governance rather than an ethical issue.

55 A

B is Absolutism, C is Consequentialism and D Utilitarianism.

56 B

Aristotle, a student of Plato, suggested this. A, Jeremy Bentham, was a classic utilitarian who believed the purpose of morality was to make life better by increasing the 'good' things. C, Kohlberg, developed the '3 levels of morality'. D, Kant believed the concept that duty is central to morality.

57 D

Whilst morals and ethics can often mean the same thing there are important differences; morals help to resolve problems with reference to individuals' personal beliefs but this does not mean that the resolution is necessarily an ethical one.

58 A

CIMA's Code is generally the same as IFAC's Code (on which it is based) but with some amendments to ensure it meets other regulatory requirements. It is not 'less stringent'.

59 A, C and D

The ethical problem that XQ faces is that a professional accountant in business should prepare or present information fairly, honestly and in accordance with relevant professional standards so that the information will be understood in its context. A professional accountant is expected to act with integrity and objectivity and not allow any undue influence from others to override his professional judgement.

XQ is facing pressure from others to change the results and therefore break the CIMA Code.

XQ is being asked to misrepresent the facts of the actual situation which would be contrary to the CIMA Code's fundamental principles of integrity and objectivity. XQ would also be breaking the due care requirement of the CIMA Code.

60 C

61 A

CIMA's Code of ethics does not give rise to a 'tick box' approach but is a requirement to practise in a certain way, setting out aspirations and standards of general behaviour. It does not lay down specific rules. The Code was launched in response to a perceived crisis in confidence in accounting generally but it was not true to say the public had lost all confidence in the profession.

62 B

It is the aim of IFAC to enhance the quality of services and develop high professional standards of accountants.

63 D

CIMA's Code reflects that of IFAC and may help to ensure ethical behaviour and it is that behaviour that may protect accountants' reputations. It may follow that if the Code is observed there may be less government intervention (as happened in the US with The Sarbanes-Oxley Act) but this possibility cannot be eliminated entirely.

64 C

Option (1) is a breach of the fundamental principle of professional behaviour and option (2) is a breach of professional competence and due care.

65 D

SYLLABUS SECTION B: CORPORATE GOVERNANCE

66 C

Fiduciary duties are relevant to the area of corporate governance and the conduct of directors. However, corporate governance is primarily concerned with matters on a broader scale related to the company and company activity, such as overall control and accountability.

67 B

Information of corporate borrowing was withheld. In order to achieve this, subsidiaries were formed. However, it was not this factor that was kept secret.

68 D

69

Rules-based	*Principle-based*
Applied in the US	Applied in the UK
Instils the code into law	Comply with the code or explain why
Penalties for transgression	Adhere to the spirit rather than the letter of the code

70 B, E

71 A

72 D

Organisations do not have to create a product or service in order to be classified as an organisation. For example, an orchestra may be classed as an organisation, but it does not necessarily create a product.

73 A

'Schools' is the correct answer because the other organisations are normally found in the private (i.e. non-governmental) sector.

74 C

C is the correct answer because this is the main activity in the public sector. Options A and B relate to the private sector.

75 A

76 B

UK Stock Exchange rules require listed companies to comply with the UK Code. Unlisted companies are not required to comply with the UK Corporate Governance Code, although it is considered best practice to do so.

There are no formal penalties for non-compliance, however the company's reputation may suffer as the result of any negative publicity.

77 B

78 C

There is an implied involvement of NEDs in the running of a company with a unitary board.

79 C

The requirements of SOX state that directors may not deal in the shares of their company at **'sensitive times'.**

If a company's financial statements are restated due to material noncompliance with accounting rules and standards, the CEO and chief finance officer must **forfeit bonuses awarded in the last 12 months.**

80 D

Recommendations on the removal and appointment of auditors are made by the audit committee

81 D

Defining an organisation is difficult as there are many types of organisations which are set up to meet a variety of needs, such as clubs, schools, companies, charities and hospitals.

What they all have in common is summarised in the definition produced by Buchanan and Huczynski. 'Organisations are social arrangements for the controlled purpose of collective goals`. Options (2) and (3) are 2 aspects of this definition but (3) is the definition of Responsible Business in the CGMA report on Managing Responsible Business.

82 A

Partnerships are one of the three common forms that a commercial organisation can take. B, C and D are all examples of NFP's.

83 D

Healthcare for the poor is an example of a Public sector organisation

84 B

In a conflict between law, ethics and corporate governance, obeying the law takes precedence. Corporate governance does not have a primary aim of getting good returns for investors and is not 'enforced' but is a system of best practice. The Conduct Committee provides oversight of professional disciplinary issues and regulation of accountants in the UK.

85 A

As a consequence of the failure of Enron (and WorldCom) the United States has introduced Sarbanes-Oxley legislation to address many of the criticisms of reporting and auditing practice. In their comments on the failure of Enron, the Association of Certified Chartered Accountants recommended the need for global financial markets to have a global set of principles-based financial reporting standards and a global code of corporate governance, arguing that legalistic, rules-based standards encourage creative, loophole based practice.

86 C

All three options are recognised reasons for supplementing the law with codes, such as The UK Corporate Governance Code.

87 A

This option is not part of Resource dependency theory but is one of the aspects of Buchanan and Huczynski's definition of an organisation.

88 False

The Sarbanes-Oxley Act is not a system of comply or explain (as is the UK Code of Corporate Governance) but of legal compliance.

89 A

This definition is not of Effective leadership and strategy; it describes Integrated governance, risk and control.

90 C

The 8 drivers are IFAC's main drivers of sustainable corporate success.

91 B

This would be the role of the upper tier, the supervisory (corporate) board. The other options are matters for the lower tier: management (operating) board.

92 D

French companies may use a unitary board or a two tier system and Germany generally favours the two tier system. The USA and UK generally favour the unitary type of board.

93 B

The Turnbull report dealt with the need for review of internal controls and The Hampel report was primarily concerned with the role and responsibility of the Non-Executive Director, and was the basis for the 1998 'Combined Code` published by The London Stock Exchange.

94 C

Section A.2 of The UK Corporate Governance Code 2010 state as a main principle, 'There should be a clear division of responsibilities at the head of the company between the running of the board and the executive responsibility for the running of the company's business. No one individual should have unfettered powers of decision. Whilst it would be good business practice to appoint a Chief Executive to take executive responsibility for the enterprise as a whole, it is not a legal requirement.

95 D

The UK Corporate Governance Code is not a legal requirement. The London Stock Exchange requires all listed companies to include in their annual reports a 'statement of compliance or non-compliance' with the code; in other words a disclosure requirement.

96 A

The Code recommends at least 3 non-executive directors on the audit committee (or 2 for smaller companies) and that half the board should be independent non- executives.

97 D

The Sarbanes-Oxley Act is part of the US regulatory framework and the Companies Act 2006 sets out the UK company law. The Cadbury report was issued by a government committee set up in response to the increased need for good corporate governance in light of several corporate scandals.

98 C

This measure is not a legal requirement under the Sarbanes Act but is within C3 of the UK Corporate Governance Code.

99 D

Codes, unlike legislation, tend to react to a problem that has arisen rather than being a proactive way of preventing a problem from arising. There can be huge differences in the size and resources of companies and globally the attitudes to good governance may differ widely.

100 B

SYLLABUS SECTION B: CONTROLS

101 A and E

An external audit does not make the financial statements error free, just free of material misstatements. The auditor will review the financial statements and advise on changes, they do not prepare the financial statements.

102 B, C, G and H

103 B

The internal audit also makes recommendations for the achievement of company objectives.

C is the role of the external auditors.

104 B

Statement (ii) is the wrong way round – external auditors test the underlying transactions that make up the financial statements, while internal auditors test the operations of the company's systems. Statement (iii) is also incorrect as internal audit is not usually a legal requirement, though corporate governance principles state that if an internal audit function is not present, the company should annually assess the need for one.

105 A

Statement (ii) is incorrect as this issue of independence would normally be an issue for internal auditors – not external auditors. Statement (iv) is also incorrect as, if the internal controls are reliable, it will reduce the amount of substantive testing that the external auditor is required to perform.

106 D

In practice many organisations find that fraud is impossible eradicate. With regards to error, as it is unintentional, it will be hard to prevent such mistakes from taking place.

In addition, there is an implied duty within an employment contract so as to encourage staff to be honest and report any actual or suspected fraud.

107 B

108 A

Stewardship is concerned with ensuring that there is a procedure in a place to safeguard assets, provide properly for liabilities, protect against misuse of assets, and report adequately to the shareholders or stakeholders of the organisation.

109 C

110 D

111 A

Part of an audit involves determining that the financial statements show a true and fair view, but it does not guarantee that this is the case; in addition, many organisations that do not have an audit performed still produce financial statements that show a true and fair view. Thus answer B is not wholly correct.

112 B

113 A, B, D

114 A, B, D, E

115

Internal Audit	External Audit
Required by shareholders	Required by statute
Reports to Audit Committee or Directors	Reports to Shareholders and Management
Reports on controls	Reports on financial statements

116 D

It is the responsibility of management to prepare the financial statements.

The auditor is required to provide reasonable assurance that the financial statements are free from material misstatement, which may include fraud.

The auditor tests a sample of balances as part of their audit work.

117 A

118 A

The internal audit function can include employees of the company, although this will limit its independence.

The internal audit function reports to management or those charged with governance.

119 C

120 D

121 D

The use of sampling is not a benefit, it is a limitation of the audit process.

122 C

Profitability is not a feature of the planning process.

123 A

The auditor should plan and perform the audit to have a reasonable expectation of detecting material fraud and error. However, if a fraud is very well concealed, even a very thorough audit may not detect it.

124 C

Financial statements cannot be verified as being correct due to the inclusion of estimates and judgements.

125 D

SYLLABUS SECTION B: CORPORATE SOCIAL RESPONSIBILITY

126 C, D, E

A strong CSR approach may, in fact, increase costs as the organisation has to source its goods more carefully. There is no reason why a strong CSR approach would speed up decision making in the organisation – in fact it is likely to use up management time that could be spent helping to earn the business higher profits. However, CSR often helps to attract both customers and staff, and reduces that chance that governments will be forced to regulate against unethical business behaviour in future.

127 A, C

The definition in B is that of CSR – not sustainability. Sustainability and CSR may cost more in the short term, but it is possible to make short-term savings. For example, becoming more energy efficient could allow an organisation to save money on fuel bills in the short term.

128 A

H is responding to demands from external groups relating to corporate social responsibility. However, he is yet to seek out ways of going beyond these requirements, indicating that he has yet to reach the proaction philosophy.

129 C, D, E

The other part of corporate social responsibility is philanthropic responsibilities.

130 NOTE: ELEMENTS CAN BE PLACED IN ANY ORDER UNDER EACH HEADING

Strategy and oversight	Execution and alignment	Performance and reporting
Board and senior management commitment	Extensive and effective sustainability training	Champions to promote sustainability and celebrate success
	Ensuring sustainability is the responsibility of everyone within the organisation	Including sustainability targets and objectives in performance appraisal

131 D

Milton Friedman argued that a corporation has no responsibilities outside of making profit pay, working conditions and job security for shareholders. Enlightened Self Interest is an argument against this viewpoint and seeks to provide an alternative view leading to the same outcome of 'profit'. All of the options are aspects of this view.

132 A

B is the perception of CSR in Ghana, C is Carroll's definition of CSR and D is the role of shareholders in corporate governance, one of the 6 principles developed by the OECD designed to assist and improve corporate governance.

133 C

Sponsoring the arts is an example of Carroll's philanthropic model of CSR.

134 B

Option (3) is Hewlett-Packard's (HP) 2006 strategy to 'Establish HP as the world's leading information technology company.'

135 D

A, B and C are some of the reasons why businesses might feel that CSR is a vital part of their strategy. D is not ; Managers have been employed in order to earn the owners of the business a return on their investment and so should act so as to maximise that return.

136 C

Procurement practices is an economic aspect of the guidelines.

137 B

(1) and (3) are from the sub category of labour practices and decent work and (2) is from product responsibility.

138 A

Option B is comparability, option C is completeness and option D is timeliness.

139 D

Shareholders and finance providers are connected stakeholders and Managers are internal stakeholders.

140 C

Employees' needs and expectations lie in pay, working conditions and job security.

141 C

The guidelines are also signed by nine non-member countries (Argentina, Brazil, Chile, Estonia, Israel, Latvia, Lithuania, Romania and Slovenia).

142 C

143 A

144 Corporations perceived as ethically sound are rewarded with extra customers.

145 C

146 D

147 B

148 The OECD guidelines for Multinational Enterprises provide voluntary principles.

149 C

150 D

SYLLABUS SECTION C: THE LAW OF CONTRACT

151 B

This was established in Fisher v Bell.

152 C

Silence cannot constitute acceptance.

153 B

This is the postal rule.

154 A

A warranty is an incidental term of the contract.

155 C

156 A

A breach of warranty means that there can only be a claim for damages.

157 C

These are essential elements of a contract.

158 A

159 A

160 B

161 A

Revocation must be communicated but does not need to be in writing.

162 B

163 C

164 A

This was established in Hyde v Wrench.

165 A

Agreement constitutes offer and acceptance.

SYLLABUS SECTION C: THE LAW OF EMPLOYMENT

166 C

There is a duty to obey all lawful and reasonable orders.

167 C

This would be an unfair reason.

168 C

169 A

The employer's intention is not a relevant factor.

170 B

This is an automatically unfair reason.

171 A

There is no implied duty to provide a reference.

172 A

Pepper v Webb.

173 C

174 C

Employment contract terms are also implied by legislation. Employees have an implied duty to obey only lawful and reasonable orders.

175 D

176 D

177 D

178 D

179 C

It is not necessary to produce documentary evidence.

180 B

A breach of contract would not be a qualifying disclosure.

SYLLABUS SECTION D: COMPANY ADMINISTRATION

181 C

182 A

183 B

184 C

185 A

186 C

Where an individual is personally liable for the business debts that person will be a sole trader.

187 C

188 A

A partnership is not a separate legal entity, whereas a company is.

189 D

The articles of association are contractually binding on members and the company only in respect of membership matters.

190 A

191 B

192 D

193 A

194 A sole trader is inappropriate for large businesses.

195 A

196 D

197 B

A formal procedure is required to dissolve a company.

198 A partnership agreement is private to the partners.

199 C

200 The articles of association regulate the relationship between the company, its shareholders and its directors.

Section 3

PRACTICE ASSESSMENT QUESTIONS

1 **Which of the following statements about The Conduct Committee (formerly The Professional Oversight Board) is correct?**

(1) It is the body responsible for establishing ethical standards relating to the independence, objectivity, and integrity of those providing assurance services.

(2) It is the body responsible for regulating specific activities of the accounting bodies regarding members' training, registration, conduct and discipline.

(3) It is the body responsible for promoting confidence in corporate reporting and governance.

A (1) only

B (2) and (3) only

C (1) and (3) only

D (2) only

2 **Which of the following fundamental principles of CIMA's Code of Ethics is defined as follows 'A professional accountant shall be straightforward and honest in all professional and business relationships'?**

A Honesty

B Professional behaviour

C Due Care

D Integrity

3 **You are the Management Accountant for a chain of fitness clubs. Your husband, who is a qualified gym instructor, has just set up in business with a rival chain and has asked you to become its finance director. Your first task is to provide him with a list of members' details from your current employer. If you supply the information would this be a breach of CIMA's fundamental principles?**

A No, as your husband is using his own skills and knows some of the members personally.

B Yes, a breach of the fundamental principle of professional competence and due care.

C No as you will not be being paid for your role as finance director.

D Yes, a breach of the fundamental principle of confidentiality.

4 The circumstances in which management accountants operate may give rise to specific threats to compliance with the fundamental principles. Which of the following statements about these threats is true?

(1) The threat that a professional accountant will be deterred from acting objectively because of actual or perceived pressures, including attempts to exercise undue influence over the professional accountant, is an advocacy threat.

(2) The threat that a financial or other interest will inappropriately influence the professional accountant's judgement or behaviour is a self-interest threat.

(3) The threat that a professional accountant will promote a client's or employer's position to the point that the professional accountant's objectivity is compromised is a conflict of interest threat.

A (1) only

B (2) only

C (1) and (2) only

D (2) and (3) only

5 Promoting shares in a listed entity when that entity is a financial statement audit client is an example of which kind of threat to the fundamental principles?

A A self-review threat.

B An advocacy threat.

C A familiarity threat.

D A self-interest threat.

6 The CIMA Code gives general guidance for handling ethical issues, both for accountants working in business and for those in practice. These safeguards may be created by the profession, legislation or regulation or in the work environment. Which of the following is not an example of a safeguard in the work environment?

A Policies and procedures to monitor and, if necessary, manage the reliance on revenue received from a single client.

B The UK Corporate Governance Code.

C Policies and procedures to prohibit individuals who are not members of an engagement team from inappropriately influencing the outcome of the engagement.

D Rotating senior assurance team personnel.

7 Which of the following statements is true?

(1) A framework based approach to developing an ethical code sets out precise guidance for each specific ethical dilemma.

(2) A rules based approach is sometimes referred to as a compliance approach

(3) A rules based approach works because it instils a sense of fear. Individuals comply because they are required to and because they fear the consequences.

A (1) only

B (2) only

C (2) and (3)

D (1), (2) and (3)

8 Which of the following is not associated with a 'framework–based` approach to ethics?

A Prevention.

B Explicit.

C Judgement.

D Discretionary.

9 Which one of the following does not need to be present in order to create a valid contract?

A Consideration

B Written evidence of the principal terms of the contract

C An intention to create legal relations

D Acceptance

10 A local newspaper advertises '40 Whizzalong scooters remaining. 3 feet high. Only £25 each'. Which legal term best describes the advert?

A Offer

B Statement of intention

C Invitation to treat

D Supply of information

11 Which of the following statements best describes consideration?

A Consideration must be adequate and sufficient

B Consideration must be adequate but need not be sufficient

C Consideration must be sufficient but need not be adequate

D Consideration need be neither sufficient nor adequate

12 Which of the following statements is correct?

A The self-review threat often results in what is commonly called a 'conflict of interest' situation.

B The main advantage of a rules based approach to ethics is that it can be applied more easily to new developments in business practice.

C An ethical framework of guidance is likely to be more wide-ranging than a fully rules based one.

D Detection is a characteristic of the framework based approach to a code of ethics.

13 Which of the following Seven Principles of Public Life is correctly described?

(1) Honesty requires that holders of public office have a duty to declare any private interests relating to their public duties and to take steps to resolve any conflicts arising in a way that protects the public interest.

(2) Objectivity requires that holders of public office should not place themselves under any financial or other obligations to outside individuals or organisations that might seek to influence them in the performance of their official duties.

(3) Integrity requires that, when carrying out public business, including making public appointments, awarding contracts, or recommending individuals for rewards and benefits, holders of public office should make choices on merit.

A (1) only

B (2) only

C (3) only

D (2) and (3) only

14 Every professional person has a duty to maintain their role of acting in the public interest by keeping themselves up to date professionally. Which of the following statements is correct with regard to the professional accountant?

A The professional accountant must be up to date with technical and professional developments because the Seven Principles of Public Life require this.

B In order to provide competent professional service, CIMA requires an accountant to attain and maintain professional competence.

C An accountant should continually develop because management accounting changes so fast that you need to keep up with it so as to stay marketable for employment.

D The fundamental ethical principle of professional behaviour requires accountants to develop and maintain their knowledge and technical skills.

15 Misrepresentation results in a contract being:

A Void

B Voidable

C Invalid

D Valid

16 X Ltd has broken one of the terms of its contract with Y Ltd. If that term is a condition, which of the following is correct?

A Y Ltd is entitled to damages only

B Y Ltd is entitled to sue for damages or to repudiate the contract

C Y Ltd is only entitled to repudiate the contract

D Y Ltd may repudiate the contract and sue for damages

17 Members of the profession need, or need to develop, certain qualities and virtues in order to meet the expectations of CIMA and the public, served in the wider context. Which of the following definitions with regard to these personal qualities is correct?

A Responsibility is the concept of being able to be trusted by others and to be dependable through the ability to deliver what and when it has been agreed.

B Reliability is the concept of delivering in a timely manner without delay and meeting the expectations of others.

C Accountability is the quality of being accountable for one's actions and decisions.

D Respect is the virtue demonstrating an attitude of esteem, deference, regard or admiration of others in dealing with them, especially where their attitudes might differ.

18 It is in the public interest, and required in CIMA's Code of Ethics that members of assurance engagement teams and their firms be independent of the assurance clients. Which of the following are the two key attributes to independence?

(1) Of mind

(2) Of belief

(3) In appearance

A (1) only

B (2) only

C (1) (2) and (3)

D (1) and (3)

19 Which of the following definitions is incorrect?

A The concept of accountability is that of the professional accountant being responsible to someone and for something or an action, and being able to explain those actions.

B Corporate Social Responsibility (CSR) is the outward manifestation of an ethical policy.

C Accountability is monitored by The International Ethics Standards Board for Accountants in the United Kingdom.

D An example of an accountant's social responsibility would be the requirement to provide accurate financial information to shareholders.

20 **Bev is employed as Management Accountant by Pretty Pictures Ltd, a small but exclusive chain of galleries. Bev has been asked to dismiss one of her colleagues for incapability but she is aware that this is not the real reason and that the company are trying to reduce the number of employees without paying the required statutory redundancy pay. If Bev tells her colleague about the real reason what fundamental principal of CIMA's Code will have been breached?**

A Confidentiality

B Integrity

C Professional behaviour

D Professional competence and due care

21 **A professional accountant should respect the confidentiality of information acquired as a result of professional and business relationships. In which of the following situations might it be appropriate for the professional accountant to disclose confidential information?**

(1) Disclosure is permitted by law and is authorised by the client or the employer: an example of this might be personal data.

(2) Disclosure is required by law, for example the production of documents or other provision of evidence in the course of legal proceedings.

(3) A professional duty or right to disclose when not prohibited by law such as when needed to comply with the quality review of a member body or professional.

A (1) only

B (1) and (2) only

C (3) only

D (1) (2) and (3)

22 Two of the world's most prestigious accounting bodies, AICPA and CIMA, are in a joint venture to establish the Chartered Global Management Accountant (CGMA®) designed to elevate and build recognition of the profession of management accounting.

Which of the following definitions is incorrect according to the recent survey by this body?

A Responsible business is about an organisation's commitment to operating in a way that is economically, socially and environmentally sustainable.

B Ethical management information allows an assessment of the organisation's ethical performance, such as the efficacy of relevant policies and procedures, occurrence of breaches of relevant policies or codes, stakeholder opinion and other metrics.

C Business ethics may include specific ethics information, such as the number of employees attending ethics training or calls to an ethics helpline, as well as routine management and risk information.

D Ethical performance applies to all strategic and operational aspects of business conduct, including sales and marketing techniques, accounting practices and the treatment of suppliers, employees and customers.

23 Which of the following is not considered to be good practice for a company wishing to implement ethical practices?

A Make conformity to the code part of a contract of employment

B Treating the code as confidential or a purely internal document

C Make copies of the code available to business partners, including suppliers

D Set up a board committee to monitor the effectiveness of the code

24 Which of the following does not constitute a duty owed by an employee towards his employer under the common law?

A A duty not to misuse confidential information

B A duty to provide faithful service

C A duty to maintain trust and confidence

D A duty to obey all orders given to him by his employer

25 Which of the following statements regarding business ethics is incorrect?

A Some typical issues in business ethics are: 'creative' accounting to misrepresent performance and corporate crime, including insider trading and price fixing.

B CIMA's Code is split into 3 parts; Part C deals with the Professional Accountant in Public Practice.

C The professional accountant may be bound by the principles of confidentiality even after the end of the relationship with a client or employer.

D The five personal qualities sought by IFAC in their International Education Standard for Accountants are: reliability, responsibility, timeliness, courtesy and respect

26 Feroz owns a newsagent, runs it as the manager and employs Ruby as part-time help during the week. Feroz is fully liable for the business' debts. What type of business does Feroz own?

A A partnership

C A sole trader

D A limited company

27 Where a professional duty conflicts with the law, which of the following options should be followed?

A The professional duty

B The law

C The professional duty if it conforms to the individuals' personal morality and ethical beliefs

D The law provided it conforms to the individual personal ethics

28 Which of the following are potential consequences to the professional accountant if a member is allowed to behave unethically?

(1) CIMA may lose its Chartered status.

(2) There may be increased regulation by government intervention.

(3) The public may lose trust in the profession.

A (1) only

B (2) only

C (1) and (2) only

D (1) (2) and (3)

29 An accountant is employed by a fashion design business but has permission to work for private clients in her spare time. She has various private clients; which of the following scenarios would not create a conflict of interest for the accountant?

A Taking on work for a company who is in direct competition with her employer.

B She has to leave her employer's premises to attend to an emergency meeting between one of her private clients and a very disgruntled creditor.

C One of her private clients asks her to work for them full time.

D The income from one of her private clients exceeds the salary she is paid by her employer.

30 On a Saturday night out at your best friend's hen party you meet one of her sisters and discover that she works for a company who designs shoes for your employer. She is very worried as she has heard that she may be made redundant as her company has no work and is making cuts in its workforce. You know that your employer is about to award them a valuable new contract. The announcement will be made first thing Monday morning. You want to put her mind at rest so everyone can have a great time.

Do you have an ethical dilemma?

A No dilemma, as she will find out soon anyway and no-one need know you have told her.

B Yes, a breach of confidentiality.

C Yes, a breach of professional competence and due care.

D No, there is no family relationship involved.

31 The finance director in your company has recently been made redundant. You have been financial controller for the last year and you are concerned that the company will assume you can take over many of his tasks. You feel that these tasks are outside your contract and you are already overstretched as the assistant to the director is on maternity leave and a locum has not been appointed.

If you feel you have an ethical dilemma which of the following things should you do?

A Nothing as you have not been asked to do anything outside your contract yet.

B Raise your concerns in writing, making recommendations of what is needed for adequate coverage of the finance director's tasks.

C Hope that the tasks will not be too onerous and that this may be the way to the promotion you have been trying for.

D Discuss the problem with your partner and ask his advice as he is finance director for a company who supply goods to your employer.

32 **Tom incorporates his sole trader business, King Kilts, which manufactured high quality tartan kilts, under the name of King Kilts Ltd. He lent King Kilts Ltd £20,000 and owns 95% of its shares. He continued to insure the company's assets, including the factory, in his own name, as he had always done prior to incorporation. On New Year's Eve, the factory was destroyed by fire. Which of the following best describes the legal position?**

A Tom can claim on the insurance because King Kilts Ltd is essentially no different from the original business

B Tom can claim on the insurance because he has an insurable interest as a creditor of King kilts Ltd

C Tom can claim on the insurance because he has an insurable interest as a member of King Kilts Ltd

D Tom cannot claim on the insurance because the insurance is not effected in the name of King Kilts Ltd and the company has the insurable interest

33 A private company cannot offer its securities to the public.

Is this statement true or false?

A True

B False

34 **Which of the following phrases best describes corporate governance?**

A Corporate governance is a set of rules by which companies are directed and controlled.

B Corporate governance is a body of rules and ethics concerned with the business efficacy and accountability of the management of publicly listed companies.

C Corporate governance is a code of best practice which, if followed, will ensure directors will be able to maximise profits for their shareholders.

D Corporate governance is the outward manifestation of an ethical policy. It states the nature of the interaction between the company and its stakeholder base, employees, customers, suppliers and so forth.

35 Which of the following statements/definitions is incorrect?

A Public interest refers to the common wellbeing or general welfare of society. Professional accountants must consider this, as they have a wider duty to act in the best interests of the public at large, as well as to the business and its owners.

B A values based approach to ethics is sometimes referred to as a compliance approach. It explicitly sets out what individuals can and cannot do, and specifies the sanctions that will be imposed for noncompliance.

C A fiduciary relationship is a relationship of 'good faith' such as that between the directors of a company and the shareholders of the company.

D CSR is the continuous commitment by business to behave ethically and contribute to economic development while improving the quality of life of the workforce and their families as well as the local community and society at large.

36 Bev Ltd placed the following advertisement in a local paper 'bargain offer, iPhones for sale latest model £5 each. Order now to get the deal of the century'

The advertisement contained a mistake; the price should have been £50. Jos Ltd immediately placed an order for 20 iPhones. Which one of the following statements is correct?

A Bev Ltd can refuse to supply Jos Ltd as the advertisement is not an offer, but a mere invitation to treat.

B Bev ltd can refuse to supply Jos Ltd but only on the condition it has sold its entire stock of iPhones.

C Jos Ltd has accepted Bev Ltd's offer and is entitled to the 20 iPhones.

D As Jos Ltd has not yet paid for the iPhones they have no contractual right to them.

37 Which of the following is correct?

(1) The parties to a social or domestic arrangement are presumed not to have intended that arrangement to have legal effect.

(2) If an agreement is of a domestic or social nature it is not possible for the parties to argue that there was an intention to create legal relations.

(3) If an agreement is in writing it is presumed that the parties intended it to have legal effect.

A (1) only

B (2) only

C (1) and (3) only

D (3) only

38 In relation to a binding contract which of the following statements is incorrect?

(1) Consideration must not be past.

(2) In certain circumstances a promise can still be binding even if both parties do not provide consideration.

A (1) only

B (2) only

C Both (1)and (2)

D Neither (1) or (2)

39 Neal Ltd has broken one of the terms in its contract with Becs Ltd. The term is a warranty, which of the following statements is correct?

A The whole contract is said to be discharged by breach but either party may elect to continue with their part of the contract.

B Terms are usually classified as conditions or warranties, a breach of a condition will only allow the injured party to end the contract, damages will not be awarded.

C Becs Ltd is entitled to damages only.

D If the court imply a term into a contract that term may only be a warranty and can never be a condition.

40 Misrepresentation may be defined as a false statement of fact or law (but not a mere expression of opinion), made by one party to the other before the contract, and made with a view to inducing the other party to enter. Which of the following statements regarding misrepresentation is correct?

A Generally silence cannot amount to a misrepresentation.

B The effect of a misrepresentation is to render the whole contract void.

C Misrepresentations may still effect the validity of a contract even if made after the contract has been concluded.

D If one party states that they will not be honouring their agreement this is a misrepresentation

41 Which of the following statements is correct?

(1) All employment contracts must be in writing.

(2) A contract of employment is not valid unless it is signed by both the employer and employee.

A (1) only

B (2) only

C Both (1) and (2)

D Neither (1) or (2)

42 The duty of fidelity is of fundamental importance in the employment contract. It is breached if, for example, an employee works for a competitor. Which of the following is not an implied duty of the employee?

A Duty to give personal service

B Duty not to misuse confidential information

C Duty to obey all the instructions of their employer

D The same duty of fidelity to an employer that they are seconded to as to their main employer

43 Which of the following is not considered to be a common law duty owed to the employee by the employer?

A To pay reasonable remuneration

B To maintain mutual cooperation, trust and confidence

C To provide work

D To take reasonable care for the safety of their employees e.g. safe plant and machinery, safe system of work and reasonably competent fellow employees.

44 Which of the following statements within employment law is incorrect?

(1) Wrongful dismissal - the term often used where the employer terminates the contract without giving proper notice, or during its fixed term.

(2) An individual who believes he has been wrongfully dismissed would sue for compensation in the form of damages (a monetary sum linked to length of the employment and the age of the employee).

(3) Summary dismissal is usually wrongful dismissal unless the employee waives their rights or accepts payment in lieu of notice or repudiates the contract themselves or is in fundamental breach.

A (1) and (2) only

B (2) and (3) only

C (2) only

D (3) only

45 Which of the following cannot justify the dismissal of an employee?

A The employee's misconduct

B The employee's incompetence

C The employee is pregnant

46 Which of the following statements about discrimination is incorrect?

A Indirect discrimination occurs when a working condition or rule disadvantages one group of people more than another, it is often illegal.

B Direct discrimination occurs when an employer treats an employee less favourably than another, due to their gender, race etc. For example, if a driving job was only open to male applicants. This is always illegal.

C Diversity is about valuing and embracing the differences in people and reaping the benefits of a varied workforce that makes the best of people's talents whatever their backgrounds.

D Employers may not discriminate against employees for joining an independent trade union or refusing to join a workplace trade union.

47 Corruption is now recognised to be one of the world's greatest challenges. Generally corruption is described as an abuse of trust in order to gain an unfair advantage. Which of the following are examples of corruption?

(1) Additional payments to induce officials to perform routine functions they are otherwise obligated to perform.

(2) The giving or receiving something of value (for example gift/loan/fee/reward or other advantage) to influence a transaction.

(3) Disclosing information that a worker believes is evidence of illegality, gross waste, gross mismanagement, abuse of power or substantial and specific danger to the public health and safety.

A All of the above.

B (1) and (2) only.

C (2) and (3) only.

D (1) and (3) only.

48 What does the UK Corporate Governance Code recommend regarding the number of non-executive directors on the board?

A They should have enough of a presence so that power and information is not concentrated in the hands of one or two individuals

B They are not required on the main board

C They should be the minority

D They should be the majority

49 What does the UK Corporate Governance Code recommend regarding the roles of chairman and chief executive?

A The chief executive should go on to be chairman at a later date

B The roles should not be combined

C The chairman's role must be performed by a non-executive director and the chief executive's by an executive director

D Individuals selected for either role must hold a professional qualification

50 What is the maximum permitted length of a director's service contract according to the UK Corporate Governance Code?

A 1 year

B 2 years

C 3 years

D 5 years

51 A two-tier board of directors comprises:

A An executive board and a management board

B A supervisory board and a management board

C A management board and a stakeholder board

D An executive board and a stakeholder board

52 Which of the following is an example of good corporate governance?

A Domination by a single individual

B Lack of board involvement

C Regular contact with shareholders

D Emphasis on short-term profitability

53 Money laundering is the process by which criminally obtained money or other assets (criminal property) are exchanged for 'clean' money or other assets with no obvious link to their criminal origins. What is the name given to the initial disposal of the proceeds of such a criminal activity?

A Failure to report.

B Tipping off.

C Placement.

D Layering

54 The case of Salomon v Salomon & Co in 1897 established which of the following common law rules in connection with companies?

A A director cannot make the decision to employ herself as CEO and then, at a later stage, bring a claim against the company for unfair dismissal.

B A director must not disclose trade secrets to a third party nor misuse confidential information he has acquired in the course of his directorship.

C A director must not request, accept or receive a bribe as a reward for performing a relevant function improperly nor use a bribe to influence a foreign official to gain a business advantage.

D A company and its members are separate legal persons.

55 Bev, Jos and Neal have decided to go into business together to run a boatyard and yacht chandlers. They call the business 'BJN boats & Co` and each invest £10,000 agreeing to share any profits equally. There is a downturn in the sailing business and they just break even in the first year but make a significant loss in the second year. They decide the business is no longer viable. Which of the following statements best describes the type of organisation?

A It is an ordinary partnership because they are in business together and intended to make a profit although they have actually made a loss.

B It is not an ordinary partnership because there is no written partnership agreement.

C It is not an ordinary partnership because it is called BJN boats & Co.

56 Bev is a sole trader, she incorporates her business designing and making wedding dresses under the name, 'Gorgeous gowns Ltd`. Bev lends the company £10,000 and owns 95% of the shares. She continues to insure the sewing unit and the hugely expensive silks and brocades in her own name. On bonfire night a stray firework caused a fire in the unit and it and all the contents were destroyed. Which of the following statements is correct?

(1) The business is a separate legal entity and must make the claim for the insurance. Bev has no legal standing.

(2) The insurance is in Bev's name and she has the right to make a claim as a creditor of Georgous Gowns Ltd.

(3) The claim will fail since the company has the insurable interest but the insurance is in Bev's name personally.

A None of the above

B (1) only

C (3) only

D (2) only

57 Being objective as an accountant is an example of:

A Contractual obligation

B Societal value

C Professional value

D Corporate value

58 Tina works for a large company as head of finance. The company has recently introduced a policy which discriminates against disabled people during the recruitment process. Tina has no moral objections to the policy and applied it when she recently filled a vacancy in her department.

This is an example of ethical tensions between which sets of values?

A Professional and corporate

B Personal and corporate

C Societal and corporate

D None – there are no ethical tensions in this scenario

59 Which of the following are fundamental principles in CIMA's ethical guidelines?

(i) Confidentiality

(ii) Scepticism

(iii) Integrity

(iv) Independence

A (i) and (ii) only

B (i), (ii) and (iii) only

C (i) and (iii) only

D All of the above

60 Which part of IFAC's code of ethics is particularly relevant to professional accountants in business?

A Part A

B Part B

C Part C

D Part D

61 Smaller Ltd is a wholly owned subsidiary of Bigger PLC. Jos ltd supplied building materials to Smaller Ltd knowing they were a subsidiary of Bigger PLC. The materials were delivered but the invoice remains unpaid and Jos Ltd has discovered that Smaller Ltd has had financial difficulties and is now insolvent. Who can Jos Ltd recover the debt from?

A The directors of Smaller Ltd personally

B Bigger PLC

C The shareholders of Smaller Ltd

D Smaller Ltd

62 Which statement best describes the ethical principle of objectivity?

A The principle of avoiding situations that may discredit the profession

B The principle of ensuring you are capable of performing the work

C The principle of avoiding the use of information obtained in the course of work for your own advantage

D The principle of impartiality and avoiding the influence of others whilst working

63 What ethical principle should CIMA members take particular care of protecting when seeking professional help to resolve an ethical conflict?

A Objectivity

B Confidentiality

C Professional behaviour

D Due care

64 You are aware that a colleague regularly takes important reports home and checks them after drinking a bottle of wine. Which of CIMA's fundamental principles are they in breach of?

A Professional competence and due care

B Objectivity

C Integrity

D There is no breach of fundamental principles

65 Which one of the following is NOT a dimension of corporate social responsibility (CSR)?

A Economic

B Ethical

C Legal

D Governance

66 When a CIMA member faces an ethical conflict, who should they look to first to resolve it?

A CIMA

B The board of directors

C Themselves

D Outside professional advisers

67 Which of the following best describes CIMA's fundamental principle of professional competence?

A Seeking help when you think that you are not suitably experienced to perform a role

B Accepting responsibility when things go wrong

C Maintaining confidentiality of sensitive information

D Refusing to take on work where there is a conflict of interest

68 Where a professional duty conflicts with the law, which should be followed?

A The professional duty

B The professional duty if it agrees with the individual's personal ethics

C The law

D The law, only if it agrees with the individual's personal ethics

69 P is a CIMA qualified accountant. He has recently attended an update course on new taxation rules that he will need to use in his current role.

Which CIMA fundamental ethical principle does this relate to?

A Professional competence

B Professional behaviour

C Confidentiality

D Integrity

70 **Which of the following is the least suitable to consult with when dealing with a major ethical dilemma?**

A A close colleague

B CIMA

C The Audit Committee of your organisation

D Your line manager

71 **Which of the following statements is incorrect?**

A An accountant should leave their job if their employer does not provide sufficient ethical safeguards

B Ethical dilemmas may be both financial and non-financial

C CIMA students are expected to demonstrate the same level as professional standards as a full members

D An accountant is always absolved from responsibility if they did not have explicit knowledge of an ethical problem

72 Corporate social responsibility (CSR) is defined as 'meeting the needs of the organisation without compromising the needs to future generations'.

Is this statement TRUE or FALSE?

A True

B False

73 It is not always a legal requirement for a company to have a strong system of corporate governance.

Is this statement TRUE or FALSE?

A True

B False

74 A misrepresentation is:

(i) A statement of fact which proves to be untrue

(ii) A statement of law which proves to be untrue

(iii) Made by one party to the other before the contract is formed in order to induce the latter to enter into the contract

(iv) A statement which affects the claimant's judgement

A (ii) and (iv) only

B (i), (iii) and (iv) only

C (i), (ii) and (iv) only

D All of the above

75 What was the mission of IFAC's Ethics Committee?

A To eliminate unethical behavior by accountants

B To develop high-quality ethical standards for professional accountants around the world

C To restore confidence in the accounting profession

D To regulate national accountancy bodies

76 External auditors have a responsibility to detect fraud.

Is this statement TRUE or FALSE?

A True

B False

77 Within the fraud response plan who will review the details of all frauds and receive reports of any significant events?

A Managers

B Audit committee

C Internal auditors

D External auditors

78 An unmodified opinion means that there are no other matters which the auditor wishes to draw to the attention of the users.

Is this statement TRUE or FALSE?

A True

B False

79 Auditors are directly accountable to the shareholders of the company

Is this statement TRUE or FALSE?

A True

B False

80 Controls testing is designed to detect material misstatement.

Is this statement TRUE or FALSE?

A True

B False

81 Substantive testing involves assessing the reliability of accounting systems.

Is this statement TRUE or FALSE?

A True

B False

82 The auditor needs to obtain sufficient evidence which relates to the quality of evidence.

Is this statement TRUE or FALSE?

A True

B False

83 The risk that a material misstatement would not be detected by the accounting and internal control systems is a detection risk.

Is this statement TRUE or FALSE?

A True

B False

84 Internal audit is a financial control.

Is this statement TRUE or FALSE?

A True

B False

85 An internal audit report does not have a formal reporting structure.

Is this statement TRUE or FALSE?

A True

B False

Section 4

ANSWERS TO PRACTICE ASSESSMENT

1 D

2 D

3 D

4 B

5 B

6 B

7 C

8 B

9 B

10 C

11 C

12 C

13 A

14 B

15 B

16 D

17 D

18 D

19 C

20 A

21 D

22 C

23 B

24 D

25 B

26 C

27 B

28 D

29 C

30 B

31 B

32 D

33 A

34 B

35 B

36 A

37 A

38 C

39 C

40 A

41 D

42 C

43 C

44 C

45 C

46 B

47 B

48 A

49 B

50 A

51 B

52	**C**	**72**	**B**
53	**C**	**73**	**A**
54	**D**	**74**	**B**
55	**A**	**75**	**B**
56	**C**	**76**	**B**
57	**C**	**77**	**B**
58	**C**	**78**	**B**
59	**C**	**79**	**A**
60	**C**	**80**	**B**
61	**D**	**81**	**B**
62	**D**	**82**	**B**
63	**B**	**83**	**B**
64	**A**	**84**	**B**
65	**D**	**85**	**A**
66	**C**		
67	**A**		
68	**C**		
69	**A**		
70	**A**		
71	**D**		